BECAUSE I'M WORTH IT

BECAUSE I'M WORTH IT

How to ask for a pay rise

Bob Stark

Get That Pay Rise

Copyright © 2023 by Bob Stark

All rights reserved. No part of this book may be reproduced or distributed in any form without prior written permission from the author, with the exception of non-commercial uses permitted by UK copyright law.

ISBN 9798375766126

Produced by Get That Pay Rise
www.getthatpayrise.com

Cover design by Wendy Brown

www.howtoaskforapayrise.com

"If you don't ask, you don't get"

Knowing how and when to ask for a pay rise is such an important skill for you to possess. It can boost your finances, change the way you think about yourself and even accelerate your career.

Having taught this skill to others, I genuinely believe it is something anyone can master. There are just a few basic rules to understand and a simple process to follow. Throw in a bit of preparation and you are ready to go.

I'm not exaggerating when I say that learning how to ask for a pay rise transformed my life. Both financially and in terms of the added confidence it gave me to speak up for myself.

My hope is that this book will give you the self-belief and the skills to do the same. So that when you do get your pay rise, you will know without a doubt that this statement is true:

You are worth it

CONTENTS

INTRODUCTION | page 1
How to ask for a pay rise

CHAPTER 1 | page 11
Why should we give you more money?

CHAPTER 2 | page 17
Playing the players

CHAPTER 3 | page 25
Make it easy for your boss to say yes

CHAPTER 4 | page 35
Replacing you isn't some cheap and easy option

CHAPTER 5 | page 41
What pay structure are you on?

CHAPTER 6 | page 53
What salary should your employer be paying you?

CHAPTER 7 | page 59
But what salary should you actually ask for?

CHAPTER 8 | page 67
Anchoring, a key tool to use in your negotiation

CHAPTER 9 | page 77
Timing is everything

CHAPTER 10 | page 81
The week before your meeting

CHAPTER 11 | page 87
Showtime: the day you ask your boss for a pay rise

CHAPTER 12 | page 105
Following up after your meeting

WHAT IF | page 109
What if... scenarios

CHAPTER 13 | page 123
How can I get more than the going rate?

CHAPTER 14 | page 129
Power words and phrases that pack a surprising punch

CHAPTER 15 | page 133
Whatever you do, don't do these

TEMPLATE | page 137
Plan of action

CHAPTER 16 | page 141
A plan is no use without the action bit

CHAPTER 17 | page 145
Troubleshooting guide

Growing up, I had a hard time unleashing the hidden power of "Don't Ask, Don't Get". I understood the concept well enough but somehow I always struggled to put it into action.

The selfless part of me knew that we had a limited family budget so it didn't seem fair to go up to my parents and ask for a Millenium Falcon for Christmas. No matter how much I might have wanted to. But I also knew that asking for things wasn't something I was very good at. A disappointing lack of natural charm probably didn't help my cause when I think back on it.

Overpriced merchandising wasn't the only thing I struggled asking about. I was so self-conscious generally that even thinking about a question would see an overwhelming anxiety kick in. Interrupting my thoughts and causing me to trip over my words. This of course meant that I stood out for all the wrong reasons at school. Anyone who has been in that position will tell you that sticking your hand up and mumbling nonsense whilst looking embarrassed doesn't mark you out as being one of the cool kids.

I get the impression that schools these days are much more supportive places but for me at the time it felt safer to simply stop asking questions in public. To only speak up if I absolutely had to. It took many years for me to become comfortable and even confident when asking questions of others. Especially if asking the question badly had potential consequences attached. That was a journey that ultimately led to my writing this book.

Back to my school days, though. If you don't ask questions you have no choice but to become more self-sufficient. So if I needed to know something, and I wasn't prepared to ask someone else, I had to gain the knowledge by other means. You couldn't Google the answer back then so that meant reading books, applying logic and becoming very familiar with solving problems. If the problem was buying something my family couldn't afford to gift me then the solution was obvious. Earn the money myself.

At fifteen I bought myself a car. Thinking ahead, I planned to fix up the crash-damaged mostly-red Renault to use once I had passed my driving test. Freedom was beckoning strongly even if it was calling from two years in the future. I would pay for it by working mornings in the local newsagent every day before school.

That part-time job in the village shop turned out to be the making of me. It was my first glimpse that life beyond the dark confines of school might prove to be a more positive experience.

Don, my boss, was a lovely man. Five foot nothing, balding and chatty, his favourite pastime was to tell me the life stories of his long-standing customers as I set up shop for the day. He quickly put his trust in me and made me feel both valued and useful.

With Don I had no choice but to start asking questions. How the till worked. Where things went. What he wanted me to do. I was nervous at first but Don would simply tell me what I needed to know and move on. This was a revelation to me. I still found it difficult but I also found it rewarding whenever I got my answer.

Fast forward a few years and I finally landed my first "proper" job having walked out of university straight into the latest recession. In between times I had taken on a string of temporary roles to keep the money flowing in. Everything from computer work at the local TV studio to running the dispatch office of a logistics firm. The aroma of subsidised cordon bleu meals in the former replaced by the odour of stale sweat and diesel from the latter. I know which I preferred. And it didn't involve forklifts. Now, though, I was starting an actual career.

It couldn't have been more different to Don's village shop. Knauf was a huge multinational manufacturer serving the construction industry. About the only thing the two businesses had in common was that they were both family-run. Though Don's family didn't take their holidays by private jet.

Knauf would prove to be a steep learning curve for me in many ways. Not least when it came to my old nemesis of anxiety when asking important questions. Like "Can I have a pay rise, please?"

I should just mention that I was a little naive at that age in my understanding of how careers were developed in practice. My assumption was this: your manager would see your work improving and your skills developing. Praise and pay rises would swiftly follow because you clearly deserved them. And repeat.

Yes, I know how that sounds. And yes, it did turn out to be a fantasy. But I hadn't had that realisation just yet so I simply concentrated on doing a better job. Learning their products, their systems and the tricks of the trade. All the while getting more capable and efficient. Patiently waiting for the day my boss would call me in to give me my pay rise. Then I patiently waited some more. As time went on I started taking on more complex work and solving bigger problems. I knew I was getting noticed because clients were now asking for me personally. My reputation was clearly growing but my salary was stubbornly staying put.

It finally dawned on me that waiting didn't work and that excelling at my job wasn't enough. The obvious solution was to ask my manager for a pay rise but what if I made a poor job of it? What if he refused or gave me the kind of feedback I didn't want to hear? So I swerved the problem and switched my efforts into looking for a better paying job elsewhere. The risk of moving to a new company felt less stressful to me than the anxiety attached to asking my boss for a raise.

I came this close to leaving until it dawned on me that the same thing would only happen again at the next company. I had to draw a line somewhere. I reasoned that if other people found the courage to ask for a pay rise then I would too. I just needed to learn how to go about it the right way. This turned out to be a smart move.

Introduction

HOW TO ASK FOR A PAY RISE

Over half of UK workers never ask for a pay rise in their entire working lives

===

That's a pretty scary statistic when you think about it. So you can take some comfort from knowing that you are far from being the only person who finds it difficult to ask for a raise. The good news is that you are now doing something about it. Your journey to asking for the pay rise you deserve has just begun.

Why do we find asking for a higher salary so challenging?

It isn't because asking for more money would be a waste of your time, that's for sure. The same Yougov survey also highlighted another important statistic: over two thirds of those who ask for a pay rise do successfully get one. You have to admit, that's a pretty good strike rate.

So why do the rest of us find the idea of it so difficult, so intimidating, so nerve-wracking?

I think a big part of it is that we can't get away from the obvious power dynamic that's in play. This can make it feel at times as if our boss is the only one who's holding any cards. That they have the freedom to act as sole judge, jury and executioner.

We also understand that companies in general don't relish the idea of their wage bill going up. And on top of that, much of our self-worth is wrapped up in our jobs and our perceived status in our role.

This makes us start to worry:

- ☹ What if we ask and get turned down?
- ☹ What if we rock the boat and then suffer forever after?
- ☹ How would we cope with the rejection?

We tend to forget there's another side to this coin

Just because they pay you, don't think for a moment that your employer holds all the aces. Yes, the company tends to be the bigger partner, but remember they are paying you for a reason.

And this means you also have power:

- ✔ Your employer really doesn't want to lose your valuable contribution to their bottom line
- ✔ Replacing staff, especially with someone who may be less capable than you, is expensive and disruptive
- ✔ Your boss is human (normally) and will have their own insecurities to consider

Even the *process* of asking can act in your favour

Your ultimate goal may be more money in your pocket but this isn't the only potential benefit on offer.

Having the courage to articulate your true worth will give an important boost to your self-confidence. Ask in the right way and you deliver a positive message about your personal development. Even if your boss turns you down this time, you will discover exactly what you need to work on in order to reach your goal.

The logic vs the reality of getting a pay rise

If simple logic was all that determined your pay then this book would be a lot shorter. Your employer would know exactly what your contribution was, your level of competence in your role, and the skillset you possessed.

They would know the market rate they would have to pay to attract and keep someone at your level (ie. the "going rate") in the type of industry and location they are based. And they would keep a watchful eye out for any of these things changing over time.

This would make sorting out your salary a piece of cake because:

- ✔ You would always be paid what you are worth
- ✔ Your employer would always be happy to pay you what you are worth

So if you could clearly show that your worth had increased then your pay would naturally follow suit without argument.

This is a perfectly logical and reasonable way of doing things. It's just a shame that real life doesn't work like that.

Why isn't real life that simple?

Because, well, because people... People are the barriers that stop this obvious and frankly fair logic from happening. People, their perceptions, their hangups and their relationships.

Companies *do* have a very good idea of how good you are, what skills you bring and what contribution you make. And it *is* straightforward to find out the going rate for what you do relative to your industry and location. But there is enough subjectivity and personal feeling involved to introduce all manner of complication.

This makes the reality of getting a pay rise more like:

- The decision to pay you the going rate is still a simple logical one for the company to make
- But it is wrapped up in a veneer of emotions (and employment law) for everyone involved

The secret is in knowing how to handle both of these aspects. And that is exactly what this book aims to teach you. Happily, the logic part is genuinely simple and the likely emotions you are going to encounter tend to be predictable and easy enough to navigate.

In this book you are going to learn how to:

- ✔ Make a clear logical case for your pay rise whilst providing the evidence to support it
- ✔ Work out the right amount to ask for
- ✔ Understand the different emotional strings to pull and how to pull them

The techniques I am going to teach you are ones that I have used successfully time and time again. They have also worked for the many colleagues and friends I have helped over the years.

It was seeing them work so consistently for so many different people in different situations that gave me the confidence to write this book. My goal is for them to work just as well for you.

Shall we get started?

How to use this book - important information

When I wrote this book I set out with the aim of helping as many people as I could. My challenge being that companies come in all shapes and sizes, as do those who are looking for a pay rise.

For all I know you could be at any point in your career from just starting out to seasoned professional. Maybe you are earning top dollar already or something closer to the minimum wage.

You could be a manager yourself, the only specialist doing what you do, or a member of a much wider team all performing a similar role to yours.

Don't worry if you don't recognise yourself in the specific examples I give because it really is the principles that matter here. You'll be adapting your approach to suit your personality and your workplace anyway, no matter what your situation.

Your very own pay rise tool box

The best way to think of this book is as a set of tools for you to choose from as you see fit. You may feel you need to use all of them or you may think that some of them aren't appropriate for your current position. Just use your own judgement.

I have included some "specialised tools" after the main chapters to help with several specific situations. For example, where your boss actually owns the company you work for. I have provided additional advice for those in this position together with a number of other useful "What if..." scenarios in their own section.

Some key points to note

As I was putting this book together, refining its content and designing its layout, I was blessed by the feedback from friends and colleagues who kindly agreed to give it the once over.

The following key points come from their questions to me about who this book was written for and how it should be used:

What salary range does this advice cover?

Pretty much any salary that you are going to earn as an employee. The principles and the basic skills that you are going to need are exactly the same no matter what your pay level.

One of the things this book is going to help you to do is determine how high your salary should really be. If that figure is less than you are on now then this book will help you to do something about it.

Does it matter where you are in your career?

As long as you are an employee receiving a salary then the techniques in this book are going to be relevant to you.

Do you have to be doing a good job?

Yes. Absolutely. There is no point looking for a pay rise using the techniques in this book if you are basically plodding along doing the bare minimum. Or if you are disruptive, on a warning or, well you get the picture. You do need to be worth the money you are looking for and you should only ask for a pay rise if you genuinely believe that you deserve one.

Does the type of company you work for make a difference?

There is a chance it will, yes. Most companies will be covered by the techniques in this book, no matter how big or small they are. But if you work in a heavily unionised sector, say the public sector, then different rules apply. You may have little freedom to negotiate your own salary unless you either earn a promotion or change employers. Even so, a good leader will strive to find a way to motivate their best staff to want to stay. And that includes pay.

When should I use my own judgement?

Always use your own judgement as to when, where, how and even if you use any of the advice or techniques in this book. If your gut is telling you that something I am suggesting will make the situation worse then listen to your gut. You are there, you know the people and you know yourself.

When should I use my own language?

Always use your own language when putting into practice the ideas in this book. I have included some example conversations and wordings to help you to get a feel for the ideas. But they are always going to sound like me. You need to be you.

Is this book only relevant to the UK?

I have written this book with just the UK and UK employment law in mind. I do understand that some readers may be living and working elsewhere in the world. This introduces differences in cultural norms, employment practices and employee protections to the challenges, none of which I am qualified to advise on. So please use your judgement on what is practical and appropriate for you to use. If your gut suggests something is a bad idea, listen to your gut.

Is getting a pay rise guaranteed?

I'm afraid nothing in life is guaranteed, especially where other people are involved. My hope is that you will be in a better place to ask for your pay rise and have a better understanding of the various dynamics involved. I want you to have grown in confidence to be able to ask in a way that leads to a positive outcome for you. Like any skill, you ultimately learn by doing, not simply by reading about it.

Before we begin

A WORD ABOUT CONFIDENCE

Confidence is simply believing that you are right. It comes from within and is difficult to fake. So concentrate on the believing bit

===

So many people mention that a lack of confidence is the main barrier that holds them back from asking for a pay rise. Even when they know for certain that they should be on a higher salary. Their heart is telling them that they deserve it but they just don't have the self-belief to say the words to their boss's face.

One of this book's jobs is to change that. Because you need to be able to show your boss that you have total faith in what you are saying. So whilst this book centres around teaching you a technique, a process for asking, it is also going to help build your confidence at the same time:

- ✔ Confidence in your own ability
- ✔ Confidence in your value to the business
- ✔ Confidence in handling your boss
- ✔ Confidence in knowing the salary you should ask for

As you read through, make notes of all the things that make you feel stronger and more in control. Remind yourself of the great work you do, the qualities you have, the contribution you make.

When you think of the day itself, remember that you don't have to get every word exactly right. You just need to be confident in your position. And to know that you truly are worth it.

Chapter 1

"WHY SHOULD WE GIVE YOU MORE MONEY?"

("they" ask)

"Because I'm worth it"   *(you answer)*

===

Just pause on that a little. Because this is exactly the angle you need to be using.

Not...   "because I need more money"

Not...   "because I know Jo's getting paid that"

Not...   "because I've been here for years and I have all these impressive qualifications"

The answer that matters is *"because I'm worth it."* And when you give that answer, or words to that effect, you need to be confident that your boss knows it's true. Getting to that point is going to form the bulk of your preparation.

Fact 1/ Companies exist to make money

And they pay staff like you to help them to do it. As a simple rule of thumb, the more your unique contribution helps a company to make money the more they will pay you in return. This is one of the many areas in life where you can directly experience and potentially gain from the rules of supply and demand.

Fact 2/ Most companies do pay their staff the going rate

Or thereabouts. If you think about it, this makes perfect business sense. The alternative would be paying your staff too little or too much. Either of which is going to cause your business problems.

Pay too little and you won't be able to hire or keep good staff. Holding on to employees who understand what they are doing is essential for any company that wants to be successful in the long-term. Without experienced staff who care about their roles you can't operate efficiently, provide a good service or generate growth. Which would make it harder for the company to make money. So paying your staff too little is simply a false economy.

Paying your staff too much, on the other hand, is going to eat into your profit margins. Leaving you less money to re-invest into the business to keep it competitive and able to grow. Less able to weather any stormy periods without laying people off. And leaving less on the table for the shareholders who own the company and want their investment rewarded. If margins are tight then paying your staff too much could cause the company to fail altogether.

So like Goldilocks' porridge, there is a sweet-spot where the salary is 'just right'. This sweet-spot is called the **going rate**.

The key question is, are you being paid less than the going rate for your *current* contribution?

This is the first thing you are going to need to work out if you want your pay rise request to be taken seriously. The going rate itself is a moving target that depends on a number of different factors, all of which are liable to change over time.

Some, such as your own skill set, are fully in your control. Whilst others, such as inflation or the wider demand for your type of work, are in the hands of the Gods.

Most of the factors involved will naturally push the going rate up over time. The exception being demand, which can go either way as technology and trends continue to develop.

The going rate for you personally has probably gone up if:

- You have taken on additional work in your role; *or*
- Your personal development means that your contribution to the business is now much higher; *or*
- The going rate for the type of work you do has risen significantly due to wider demand

Any one of these is going to give you a great opportunity to ask for, and get, your pay rise. As well as putting you in a position to be able to justify it in terms that your company will understand and see as fair and reasonable.

I'm now going to point out something obvious

This should go without saying really. But you do have to be good at your job if you want to ask for, and expect to receive, even a small pay rise.

By the same token, if you want a pay rise that's "a bit special" then you need to be doing something "a bit special" to earn it. And if you are after an "exceptional" pay rise you really do need to be exceptional in your role.

Not necessarily exceptional at everything. But you do need to be bringing something extra of value to the party and there is no point kidding yourself otherwise. Especially if other people in your company are performing the same role that you are.

Why? Because the alternative is that you are just doing the same job to the same standard as everyone else. And expecting to get paid more money than they are isn't going to sound fair to anyone.

So, your first task is this:

- ✔ Be clear on what it is that has changed that means the contribution you personally make to the business is now worth more money to your employer

This is the core material that you are going to be building the conversation with your boss around.

BECAUSE I'M WORTH IT

Chapter 2

PLAYING THE PLAYERS: UNDERSTAND THAT WE ARE ALL DRIVEN BY SELF-INTEREST

Get a feel for the key players, what it is that drives them, and why all this matters

===

You may feel tempted to skip this chapter and get straight to it but let me warn you: ignoring the needs of the key players is the single biggest mistake I see people make. Don't let it be yours.

But surely this is about me, not a bunch of "key players"?

The thing is, what you want is obvious to everyone: "*more money, please.*" But the decision-makers in your company aren't going to base their decisions on what *you* want. They care far more about what *they* want. We need to switch your boss's mindset from "*why should I give it to you?*" to "*why wouldn't I give it to you?*" The key players in your company can all influence that change in attitude.

Meeting your "customer's" needs

When you ask for a pay rise you take on the effective role of a salesperson. A salesperson with just a single product to sell - that "product" being you. The trouble is, your employer already has access to that product and at a price they are used to paying. You therefore need to help your "customer" to understand how paying a bit more for you is actually going to be in their best interests.

A good salesperson will look at their customer's drivers and deliver a sales pitch that meets their needs. They identify potential objections and come prepared to tackle them. They make sure that they are in a position to show their product off in the best light.

So with that in mind, let's take a look at each of the key players and what their individual needs and potential objections are.

Key player - Your Boss

Your boss is the first and most obvious key player to understand. As well as being the most important, given they are likely to be the one you will be asking directly for a pay rise.

Being your boss they should know you pretty well. You would expect them to have formed a clear picture of how capable you are and the contribution you are currently making to the company. If you have been developing well in your role they may also have a view on how far you could go in the future.

The more direct influence and autonomy your boss has in the company, the less you have to worry about any of the other players.

What does your boss really want?

Honestly, more than anything, they probably just want an easy life. Most of us do. But beyond not having to add to their own workload let's look at some typical drivers. *They will care about:*

- How their own boss and other key staff perceive them
- Maximising their team's performance
- Meeting any targets they have been given
- Not losing their best staff
- Keeping their team's motivation high
- Maintaining their team culture
- Feeling in control
- Not being seen by others as weak
- Feeling good about themselves

There are plenty of positive levers in that list that you can use to help your case. We'll get to those in the next section, which is wholly dedicated to handling your boss.

But there are also a few potential hurdles to watch out for:

- Your boss won't want to be seen as weak
- They need to feel in control at all times
- Their targets may include a limit on salary increases
- They care deeply how they are perceived by others

So what does all this mean for you? In order to give yourself the best chance of getting a "yes" you are going to need to navigate a path around these hurdles. This is why the way you go about asking your question and the choice of words that you use both matter so much.

It is also why you are going to need to do a little bit of preparation and setup work beforehand.

Part of that preparation is going to involve you proactively finding ways to:

- ✔ Allow your boss to keep feeling strong and in control
- ✔ Ensure your boss is seen that way by the other key players
- ✔ Bypass any salary limit targets they may have been set

As you read through the rest of this book I am going to share some tools and language with you that are designed to do just that.

Key player - Your Boss's Boss

Unless your boss is actually the CEO or owns the company themselves (see page 119 if they do) they are unlikely to be the sole decision-maker when it comes to your pay rise. At the very least they are going to have to answer to *their* boss.

Whose own drivers are going to be very similar if not identical to those of your boss. But at a higher level of responsibility and hence a higher level of reputational risk for them to worry about.

The key point being this: your boss is going to have to justify your pay rise to *their* boss. And to do that they need to be able to offer a more detailed explanation than a simple "they deserve it."

A couple of key questions for you

- How well does your boss's boss know you?
- What opinion do you think they have of you?

I'm going to assume here that your boss enjoys a good relationship with their own boss (if they don't, then take a look at the troubleshooting guide on page 145).

A positive answer to the above questions is great news and should give you extra confidence to press forward. And anything non-committal is unlikely to cause you any problems.

The only real issue would be if your boss's boss already has a low opinion of you. If you think this is likely then you are going to have to spend a little more time on your preparation. My advice here would be to go and see your own boss and discuss your concerns openly with them. Ask them what "we" need to do to help the situation and then ask for their support in resolving it.

Key player - HR Manager (if you have one)

In my experience, there are a lot of misconceptions around HR's role when it comes to handing out pay rises. In truth, they are rarely the ones who hold onto the purse strings or make the final decisions on salaries.

What they do hold onto, and insist on applying as rigorously as possible, are the various rule books when it comes to pay. These include the company's own set of rules and norms and all the relevant employment law that applies. HR teams like to have rules. And they like them to be applied consistently.

This need for consistency can be a problematic hurdle (that we will tackle later) when you ask for a pay rise just for yourself.

To give you a flavour of some of the more problematic things an HR department won't like:

- Do you have a poor attendance record?
  (HR won't want you to be rewarded for it)

- Do you have the same job title as 5 others?
  (HR won't want your pay to be different to theirs)

- Have other people had pay rises refused recently?
  (HR won't want yours accepted)

None of these problems is going to be insurmountable with a bit of creative thought. But you should be aware that your boss may have their work cut out in tackling them if they do exist.

At the very least they are going to have to have some additional conversations. And the better prepared your boss is, the easier it will be for them to clear this hurdle for you.

Try to head off issues like these directly with your boss

If you think any of these are relevant to your situation:

- A poor attendance record
  Convince your boss it is a thing of the past and prove it

- The same job title as others
  Show why you are exceptional, or suggest a new title

- Other people have had pay rises refused recently
  "I am an individual and I think I have a strong case"

Is there any good news when it comes to HR?

Actually, yes there is. Being a stickler for consistently applying the rules is one of the many reasons why you shouldn't fear the very idea of asking for a pay rise. More on that later.

Part of HR's role is to provide reports to the company's senior management team. We are talking metrics like attendance records and sick days taken, as well as staff turnover and recruitment costs.

Your boss will be well aware that high staff turnover and having to pay recruitment fees to find replacements will be seen as a negative indicator against their department's performance.

Or in other words, whilst there may be a cost to giving you a pay rise there may also be unwanted consequences should you decide to leave because your request was turned down.

What if you work for a small business?

In smaller companies you will often find a single person taking on the roles of both accounts and HR. How much influence they have normally depends on how close their relationship is with the company's owner. It may be that you don't have to concern yourself with them but use your own judgement on this.

Key player - Finance Director (if you have one)

The Head of Finance, unlike the HR department, really does hold the purse strings. They set the department budgets to keep the company on-track and solvent. Among those budgets is payroll, typically one of the biggest cost centres in any company. So a department head who tries to push their payroll over budget can expect to receive a difficult call.

What this means for you is that your boss may be seriously constrained by their payroll budget. The Finance Director could say to them: *"there's no money available for raises right now"*. This is obviously a hitch but in most cases it won't be insurmountable.

I have found over the years that Finance Directors tend to be both pragmatic and logical individuals. They understand the value of good staff and this means they can normally be convinced to make an exception if you can provide clear enough evidence.

Your options here are going to include:

- Gently pointing out to your boss the potential risks (and costs) to the company of not giving you a pay rise
- Waiting for a better moment to ask for your pay rise

We will cover both of these in more detail later.

What if your company really is on the rocks?

Sadly, sometimes the message *"we have no money"* is a genuine sign that your employer is in real trouble. If you think this might be the case then you should ask yourself if staying put is really the best idea.

Chapter 3

MAKE IT EASY FOR YOUR BOSS TO SAY "YES"

Your boss is like a lock on the door to your pay rise. Here is your key to opening it

===

I want you to take a nice slow deep breath. Open your heart as wide as you can. And do your best to feel a little empathy for your boss when you read this section. Yes I really do mean that.

You don't need me to tell you that asking for a pay rise is not something most of us look forward to doing. But trust me when I say that your boss doesn't enjoy having these conversations either.

If you want to know why that is, try putting yourself in their shoes for a minute:

- As a manager, if you say "*yes*" to a pay rise you are going to have to hold a series of conversations with the likes of the CEO, FD, and HR. Each of whom will want you to justify your decision to them. This is a pain and comes with risks.

- If your wider team finds out it could trigger a whole host of copycat requests. Followed by a series of difficult conversations leading to a much less happy team.

- If you answer "*no*", even if totally justified, it risks damaging your relationship and reducing the motivation and performance of your valued member of staff.

- If the conversation goes really badly you could end up losing your valued team member altogether. And then you have to deal with all the subsequent disruption and hassle.

When I was a boss I used to hate these conversations when they came out of the blue. My heart would immediately sink because if their pay rise request was justified it meant I had failed to keep up with my team member's development. My philosophy was always to pay the going rate for a role and I didn't wait to be asked to hand out a deserved salary increase.

On the other hand, if they were wide of the mark in their view of their own performance I was going to have to find a constructive way to let them down gently.

Clearly, it was a far more pleasant conversation when I could answer "yes". But it still meant a lot of my time would be consumed with sorting out all the details.

Importantly, if I was going to be able to give my team member the answer they wanted to hear then I had to be certain that it was the right thing for me to do.

The next few pages are going to show you how to make it easy for your boss to support you. We want them to know instinctively that "yes" is the obvious answer they should give to your request for a pay rise.

Does your boss also own the company?

If they do then don't forget to read the additional section "What If Your Boss Owns The Company" on page 119.

1/ Your actions will speak louder than words

To make it a no-brainer for your boss to say "yes" to your pay rise request there needs to be zero doubt in their mind that you are worth the money that you are asking for.

Telling them how good you are is one thing but if you want your boss to believe you, you really need to be walking the walk.

Which means:

- ✔ Doing great work that shows your true value to the business *before* you ask for your pay rise

- ✔ Demonstrating all the positive qualities that you are going to be using to support your case

- ✔ Doing this so consistently that your boss, and everyone else around you, can't fail to notice

The brighter you shine, the easier it is going to be for your boss to answer "yes", confident in the knowledge that justifying it to others is going to be a piece of cake.

2/ Start thinking W.I.I.F.Y.B.
What's In It For Your Boss?

As humans we are creatures driven primarily by our own self-interest. You only have to ask yourself why you want your pay rise. And you know what? Your boss is no different to anyone else. Their self-interest is the key motivator you should be appealing to.

This is why it is so important that you make an effort to understand what your boss's drivers really are. Ask yourself how the contribution you are making can specifically help your boss with the things that matter most to them.

List down a few ideas and start to put a plan into action. To see if it is working, take a moment every so often to check if your boss has noticed any changes you have made. Don't obviously fish for a complement but try along these lines instead:

"I've been doing <this thing> to try and improve <that situation>. Do you think it's having any effect? Is there anything you think I should try instead?"

3/ Use numbers to make your worth tangible

You may think it should be obvious to your boss just how much you are worth. I mean, look at all that great work you are doing. Of course they're going to know how good you are.

The problem is *"how good"* and *"great work"* are both subjective. They are only opinions. Positive opinions for sure, especially if your boss shares them. But hard facts are a whole lot better. And this is where numbers come in.

Because business really is a numbers game:

- How much money are we spending?
- How much profit are we making?
- How can we get 10% better at it?

When you can use numbers to show how your unique contribution is making a difference to the business you suddenly have a very powerful tool. One that plays to both the logical and the emotional elements of your boss's decision-making process.

The logical aspect because if you have just saved the company £100K due to the great idea you implemented then suddenly a £7K pay rise doesn't seem such a big ask.

And the emotional aspect because your boss now has some hard facts they can proudly tell others about. Numbers, especially financial ones, are the universal language of business. Your boss can use positive numbers to look good in front of literally *anyone*.

So take a good look at the additional contribution you have been making. Any special projects you have completed or little improvements you have made. And try to work out what that extra something is worth financially to the business when compared to someone who is "just doing the job".

Then try mentioning these figures to your boss. Ask them if this is the kind of thing they'd like to keep seeing from you.

What if you are struggling to calculate what your extra something is worth financially?

If you don't have that experience yet then don't worry. It may even strengthen your relationship with your manager when you ask them to help you to work it out.

My advice here is not to overcomplicate things. You aren't suddenly asking to see the company's profit and loss accounts. You are just trying to put a pounds and pence figure on the impact that your project or idea has made.

Tell your boss you are sure it has made a measurable financial difference. But you don't know how to go about working the exact figure out. Can they help you as you are interested to know?

Any decent boss will be impressed that you are seeing the bigger picture around your work. And once they've spent their time helping you to work out the numbers, you can be sure they are going to stand by them when you bring them up in the future.

'Star' employees are often taken for granted

As a manager, it's easy to overlook the value added by your star members of staff. Even though you know how good they are, you stop noticing all the important things they do because they just quietly take care of stuff before it hits you.

This can be just as true for the 'Stars' themselves. You can forget that what you are doing is special simply because it has evolved to become part of your normal day job.

Common ways star employees add overlooked value:

- ✔ Defusing and turning around unhappy clients
- ✔ Training and mentoring other team members
- ✔ Creating technical workarounds
- ✔ Sourcing cheaper suppliers or products
- ✔ Solving disputes between departments
- ✔ Finding new efficiencies in processes
- ✔ Reducing waste and breakages
- ✔ Taking on work that doesn't fit an existing role
- ✔ Producing a higher output than their colleagues

If you are adding value in ways your colleagues aren't, or that can't realistically be expected of just anyone doing your role, then that added value is worth bringing up.

Putting a ££ value to your extra contribution

Example 1: Reducing Wastage

You found a way to double the life of the specialist tool you use from 1 month to 2 months by changing how it is used.

You taught the 5 other members of your team to use the same method. Each replacement tool costs £735

Saving = 6 tools every 2 months at £735 per tool

Per year = 6 (tools) x 6 (periods) x £735 = £26,460

Example 2: Emergency Technical Workaround

A new product launch nearly went horribly wrong because it was incorrectly set up in the software you use.

You are part of the sales team and quickly realised the problem. You know the system well and created a workaround that enabled your team to take customer orders until the problem was fixed properly the next day.

Your team took 330 orders at £130 per order and you have been told your company makes 15% profit each time. You also estimate you saved 30 complaints; each would cost £500.

Value = 330 (orders) x £130 x 15% (profit) = £6,435
plus saving 30 (complaints) x £500 = £15,000

Total Value = £6,345 + £15,000 = £21,345

4/ Make supporting you one of your boss's own personal goals

I know that some don't always show it but your boss really is going to have a heart, an ego and feelings. And in an ideal world you want to have all three of them to be working passionately for you.

Sounds unlikely? You'd be surprised. Especially if you are someone who generally makes your boss's life easier rather than giving them a new headache to deal with every day.

There are two things that make this outcome far more likely:

- If your boss feels a sense of personal pride in how you have grown your contribution to the business

- If your boss believes that your motivation is only going to increase further if they give you a pay rise

It's even better if your boss genuinely likes you as a person. But their liking you won't be enough on its own. Don't forget that they still have to be in a position to credibly justify your raise to the other people in the business.

How to instil a sense of personal pride in your boss:

- ✔ Let them know just how much you appreciate all the help and support that they give you

- ✔ Ask them for their recommendations for things like books and courses and give them positive feedback when they do

- ✔ Show a genuine interest whenever they share their techniques and experience with you

- ✔ Ask them for their feedback on your performance regularly and act on it in a way they can see

A note of caution: When you start mentioning pay rises, your boss is going to have one eye on your future motivation

This is especially true if you have only recently upped your game.

The reason for this is that your boss will worry that your current effort may just be some temporary blitz. That your only motivation in working to this level is to bag yourself a pay rise. As soon as you get one you, they think, you might slow back down to your previous level.

You need your boss to know that this isn't the case. That in fact you are on a genuine journey of growth and this is what they are seeing whenever you show them another piece of your great work.

The simplest way for you to do this is to talk to your boss about your future ambitions. Asking for their help in getting you to the level you want to be is an even better tactic as it plays again into that sense of personal pride.

Leaders love to feel that they are helping others to develop. It really does motivate them and gives them energy. If you can play into that then both of you end up walking away with a win.

I can tell you from my own personal experience that developing others soon became the single most important aspect of my role to me. Looking back, this is the part of my career that I am easily the most proud of.

Chapter 4

REPLACING YOU ISN'T SOME CHEAP AND EASY OPTION

Hiring someone new would be expensive, risky and disruptive. Great news for you!

===

Why is there a section on the problems of replacing you?

A lot of people genuinely worry that they may get sacked for just requesting a pay rise. That somehow the question will so incense their boss that their first reaction will be to lash out and fire you.

I am telling you now that I cannot imagine a sane boss ever doing this to a valued employee. Believe me when I say that replacing a productive member of staff is rarely a cheap, easy and smooth process. In fact it's normally quite the opposite.

Even if your boss isn't sane, most countries have a host of employment laws to stop this happening anyway. In the UK, short of gross misconduct, your HR department would almost certainly be on your side should your boss try it. As would the law after two years' service.

So this section is included purely so you can understand the costs and problems your boss would face if trying to replace you. Have a read through, then confidently put that thought to bed and get back to concentrating on the important stuff.

Hiring new staff is a royal pain in the a**e

If you have ever tried to recruit new talent you will know just how long the whole process can take. It isn't just finding the right person that takes time, it's all of the other crap you have to go through as a manager: writing ads and job descriptions, holding interviews, notice periods, paperwork, inductions, training.

And that's just for starters. After that comes all the oversight needed to get your new hire up to full competence.

In the meantime the rest of your team is busting a gut trying to take up the slack, which inevitably causes its own issues. Even then your new hire may never be as good as the person who left. This is why no company wants to lose a good member of staff.

I'm not suggesting that you take the "pay me or else I leave" approach. Or that you consider yourself either indispensable or irreplaceable. But you can be sure that the risk of you leaving if you don't get what you want will be playing on your boss's mind.

The direct costs of hiring are what get reported

Advertising a role isn't actually that expensive to do. In fact some job sites let you do it for free. The problem with this is that you get zero quality control before the applications hit your inbox.

You have to read through all the CVs yourself, make a longlist, then a shortlist, and organise all of the admin. It can be massively time-consuming, particularly if the role looks enticing to lots of candidates. This then pushes up the indirect costs enormously.

The alternative is for the company to use a recruitment agent. The direct costs are a lot higher this way but using a good agent will remove some of the indirect pain.

Recruitment agents typically charge 10-20% of a candidate's first year salary. So hiring for a £40K position would cost the company £4K-£8K, depending on the rate that was agreed.

As with most things in life you tend to get what you pay for with a recruitment agent. Specialist headhunters will charge more. Whilst an agent who is easily beaten down on price will likely cut corners when vetting candidates. Time is money, after all.

But the indirect costs are much higher

This rarely gets discussed in businesses let alone calculated. It just seems to be accepted as a necessary evil. But hiring, even when using a recruitment agent, is hugely time consuming.

To make it worse, the people whose time is vacuumed up tend to be the more expensive members of your staff: the managers.

Try putting their hourly rates against:

- The hours spent reading through CVs and agreeing on a shortlist

- Then booking and holding the interviews

- And then again with second interviews

- Followed by all the paperwork that's involved with a new starter

- And, once they start, running the inductions, the IT setup, training, settling the new hire in etc.

All those hours would rapidly add up in lost productivity for your boss, your team and the HR department. Not to mention the lost output from being a team member down.

Even once they have got up to speed the new starter still won't have all your experience and knowledge of the business. The bottom line is this: they still won't be you.

Tell me, what's your best guess as to what it would cost the business if your role wasn't fully delivered for 6 months or more?

What about the risks of hiring someone new?

The more unique and business-critical your role, the bigger the risk to the company if you leave. This is especially true if your role is considered essential to their future development plans.

Not only will you know stuff that no-one else does but your team will have got used to the way you go about doing things. All of which makes replacing you that much harder and the likely disruption more serious. This is one of the many good reasons to carve out a unique position for yourself, by the way.

If yours is a role that many others also do at your firm then the number of unknowns is going to be lower. Your employer will already have a reasonable idea of how difficult it is to recruit for. How long it is likely to take before a new hire is fully up to speed and being productive. And how much all that will cost.

The team dynamic is going to change

To be fair, it could get better. But there is a very real risk it could get much, much worse without you in the team. Sometimes the roles that different people play in motivating and supporting each other in a group are blindingly obvious. Often, though, you only find out when someone leaves that they were the glue that has been holding the dynamic together.

Let's assume that you generally get on fine with your colleagues. You work well together, you know each other's habits and you are comfortable and settled as a team. Your boss will know that if you leave then that dynamic, and with it the performance of the team itself, is going to be under threat.

This adds yet another dimension to trying to find the right person to replace you. Any sensible hiring manager these days knows that they have to consider team-fit as one of the key attributes they are looking for in a candidate.

But if they get it wrong and their new hire doesn't fit in or, worse, turns out to be actively disruptive:

- Productivity and team morale will quickly start to suffer

- Key projects will start to slip as the team becomes dysfunctional

- Your boss will be forced to spend precious time getting involved to try to fix the issue

- Before long the company's bottom line is being affected

- Quickly followed by your team's (and your boss's) reputation

When new hires don't work out you need to act quickly and decisively to minimise the damage. Before going back and starting the whole painful and time-consuming hiring process again.

Hopefully you can now see how much hassle and disruption is involved in finding and onboarding a new member of staff when someone leaves. This level of pain really isn't something a company, or your boss, will take lightly. So please put that thought to bed and get back to preparing to ask for your pay rise.

Chapter 5

WHAT PAY STRUCTURE ARE YOU ON?

An inflexible pay structure can be used as an excuse by your boss. Here's how to handle the most common situations

===

Nearly every company, once it reaches a certain size, will start to introduce pay structures into the mix. These provide consistency and control for the business whilst also presenting a shiny veneer of fairness to staff. As they mean introducing a new set of rules, you won't be surprised to hear that HR departments love them.

A typical defined pay structure is what you might call a mixed blessing. On the one hand you can take some comfort from knowing that a lot of thought will have gone into your salary. On the other hand, many defined pay structures seriously restrict your ability to negotiate a raise when you believe you deserve one.

This is because your boss can simply refer to the pay structure, put on their sad face, and tell you that their hands are tied. Sorry and all that. And in fairness to them, they may well believe it.

In my experience there is nearly always a way around the restrictions that have been designed in. But you do need to be realistic about the challenges that structured pay regimes present.

Still, challenging or not:

- ✔ If you are special at what you do; *and*
- ✔ If your boss is motivated to help you

Then it's amazing how often a handy loophole in the rules can magically appear.

Fun fact: the larger the company the more rules there tend to be around salaries

Whilst in smaller organisations there are often few or no formal salary structures in place. The business may not even retain a full-time HR role yet as the number of staff they employ wouldn't justify the expense. In small companies like this the business owner is likely to be directly involved when it comes to pay rise decisions. Even if they aren't your direct boss, their opinion of you is therefore going to matter.

This relationship between having fewer rules and not having an HR department almost certainly isn't a coincidence. And there are both upsides and downsides for you to consider here.

Having fewer rules allows your boss more flexibility to design a happy outcome when you come looking for more money. But it's worth remembering that some of the restrictive rules that HR insist on are designed to work in your favour and to protect you.

Another fun fact: the more senior or specialist your role the less these rules are going to apply to you

This is a bit of an unspoken rule and your HR department won't want to admit to it. It doesn't stop it from being true, though.

What you will find is that if your contribution is both unique and highly valuable to the business then the way you are treated will tend to reflect that.

My experience is that, even in the largest of companies, a supposedly rigid pay structure can be "tweaked" or even a new structure introduced in order to keep a vital employee happy.

Over the next few pages we will take a look at some common pay structures. As well as showing you what you can do to work around them

1/ Set pay within structured competence bands

We'll start with what is probably the hardest system to approach on an ad-hoc basis. Competence bands are specifically designed to stage-manage pay requests by giving staff a clear ladder to climb.

"You'd like a pay rise? No problem - here's the list of all the competences you need to reach the next band."

On the upside, these structures are normally clear, fair and transparent. Which is why HR departments like them so much. Their achilles heel is that the competence list that your HR team has so carefully compiled can't possibly cover every single aspect of what you do. Which is where the handy loophole appears.

Because in real life most people's roles are far more nuanced than a simple list can describe. Sometimes HR will add a little wiggle room into the salary bands in order to accommodate this reality. If yours has done this and the pay rise you are after is within that range then perfect - you don't have a problem.

But if each band has a rigidly fixed salary amount, or you are looking for a rise beyond the band, then you need to get creative.

My advice would be:

Demonstrate that a chunk of the work that you uniquely do isn't covered within the band descriptions

Explain that you don't want to stop doing this important extra work. But you feel it is only fair that your pay reflects the reality of your specific contribution to the business.

One option you could suggest to resolve the problem is that you be removed from the band structure by taking a different job title. Or you could ask for a separate 'Added Responsibility' pay on top of the band to reflect the extra contribution you are making.

2/ Annual % increase for all employees

The basic principle here is as simple as they come. Everyone in the company gets the same % pay increase and you all receive that increase on the same day.

This has a lot of advantages for the company as it makes budgeting and payroll nice and easy to manage. It also means that a single company-wide announcement can be made, saving everyone time. Managers can say it is fair and point to the fact that they have got exactly the same increase as you.

This is actually a nice structure to be in from a negotiating point of view. Because there are few hard rules to worry about, you still have a lot of freedom to ask for the pay rise you want. As long as you get your timing right.

You also have the basic principle locked in that salaries should go up naturally over time.

My advice would be:
Time your request well away from the annual increase date

I'm going to suggest that you ask for your pay increase at least two months before or two months after the normal annual increase date. That way you force your boss to look at it as a wholly separate thing to the standard process. They can't then use the annual increase as some kind of bargaining chip or blocker.

You need to be making the point that something has changed that means your salary should be looked at *now*, from a whole fit-for-purpose perspective. It's not that you are unhappy with the company increasing everyone's salaries every year. In fact, you think that is a good thing in its own right.

3/ Managers are given a pay rise budget to deploy amongst their team once a year

This is a very common system in larger companies and one that is rightly despised by the managers who have to implement it.

The way it works is this: each department head is given a fixed budget to cover all the pay rises for their team. It's entirely up to them how they share this money out. They can reward some members of their team with bigger increases and give less to others. Whatever they think is best. The timing of the pay rises will be the same for every employee in the company.

It often isn't made clear to staff that it is actually their manager who has decided the pay rise they are getting this year. But it is nearly always left to the manager to give out the good or bad news.

This structure is cleverly presented to managers as being empowering because it gives them complete "flexibility and control" over their team. But don't be fooled.

This is a horrible trap for your boss

Why is it a trap? Well, think about it. Everyone in your team knows exactly when pay rise time is. So let's assume that you have been doing a fantastic job and both you and your boss know it. Come pay rise time you are going to be feeling pretty confident that you're due a decent raise.

Your boss is thinking the same thing. They want to do something special for you so off they go to their boss to get an increase to their budget signed off.

"*It's no problem*" they are told, "*you know your budget. Just work out who you want to disappoint.*"

Yep - with this system you only win if one or more of your colleagues loses in order to cover the difference.

So now your boss has a difficult choice to make:

- Give you a lower raise than they wanted to and deal with the fallout from your disappointment; *or*
- Give you the raise that you deserve and deal with your colleagues when some of them get nothing at all

I absolutely hated this system when I was forced to use it as a manager. Honestly, I would waste days trying to work out the best overall compromise and how to pitch it to everyone.

All the time knowing that the best I could hope for was only mild disappointment from most of my team.

My advice would be:
Time your request well away from the annual increase date

Here's a top tip if you are confident that this is the structure that is in place at your company. Because you have a golden opportunity to help your boss, assuming they hate it as much as I did.

Tell your boss that if you get the salary increase you are asking for now, well away from the annual increase, that you won't expect an additional pay rise this year when that time comes around again. This will give your boss the chance to use your share of their annual pay rise budget to better reward one of your colleagues.

You obviously need to do your maths and make sure that the raise you are asking for is significant enough for you to come out on top. But if it is, then this could be a rare opportunity for your boss to be in a position to make everyone happy for once.

4/ Basic plus significant bonus / OTE

This structure is traditionally associated with sales, although lots of roles include some form of variable bonus payment on top of a basic salary. Bonuses are designed, or should be, to motivate you to do certain things as a priority by rewarding specific outcomes.

Unfortunately, many bonus schemes are seriously flawed beasts. Creating more friction in practice than they do any desired outcome. That doesn't stop companies wanting to incorporate a bonus scheme into their salary packages, though. Mainly because the "carrot and stick" principle they provide is so easy to apply.

It is important that you understand that a bonus isn't a guaranteed form of income, nor are they a protected part of your salary. A company can choose to stop or change a bonus scheme much more easily than trying to reduce someone's basic wage.

The other benefit they offer a company is by providing an easy get-out clause for your boss should you ask for a pay rise:

"You'd like a bigger salary? No problem, you just need to work harder to earn a bigger bonus."

My advice would be:

Don't fall for the "earn more bonus" approach - but do be ready for it

Explain that you are asking for a pay rise because your current contribution is *already* worth more than you are being paid. That it isn't you or your efforts that need to change. It's your rate of pay that does to reflect the going rate for what you are already doing.

One upside of having a bonus scheme is that it does give you some flexibility to get creative, assuming your company allows it:

- Would you prefer an increased basic salary?
  (with the same bonus package on top)

- Should the rate of the bonus be increased?
  (which may be more acceptable to the company)

- Should the basis of the bonus change?
  (ie. does the bonus reward the right things)

You can often have an interesting and open discussion with your manager around these different options. Try to find a solution that works well for both you and the company.

Maybe ask your boss what they are really trying to achieve with your bonus and see if you can suggest a better alternative to get that result for them.

Note: some companies actively misuse bonuses

A bonus is defined by the Merriam Webster dictionary as "*Something in addition to what is expected*". Used in this way a bonus scheme can be a great motivator to drive extra performance.

Some companies, though, start each month with your bonus already in place. Provided you don't make any mistakes or break any equipment or have a day off sick or whatever else they think of then that bonus is yours come pay day.

Reality? Something always happens and the bonuses are rarely paid. This isn't a bonus scheme. It's a punishment scheme.

Companies that run bonus schemes like this either don't understand how to motivate their staff or they don't care to try.

5/ Commission-only pay

It takes guts to accept a commission-only role because you are the one taking all the risks. Which should also tell you something about the likely mentality of your employer. If you aren't performing then don't bank on them looking after you.

My first question for you if you are in this position is: are you one of the top earners in your role? If you are and you have been consistently then you've got some leverage to work with.

A couple more questions for you:

- What was it that made you take on a commission-only position in the first place?

- Why did your employer only offer a commission-only salary for this position?

The answers to these should give you some clues as to how your boss may react when you ask for a raise.

My advice would be:

Be very clear on your true value to the company and the unique skills and experience that you offer them

Companies with this mindset tend to be very focused on your immediate value to their bottom line. If you know the profit (not just sales) you are generating then you can use this to make a strong case for yourself.

Cold, hard numbers are the way to go in this situation

When you get to discussing your raise with your manager you will typically have two options to base your negotiations around:

- Asking for a higher paying commission-only model
- Trying to move to a more secure basic-plus-bonus setup

The more challenging of the two will normally be the move to a basic-plus-bonus setup. This is because your employer will want to be confident that you won't lose your edge with a basic-pay safety net in place.

Good reasons to give include: to enable you to secure a mortgage or loan (where only guaranteed income is taken into account), or simply for your own self-esteem. The one answer they really don't want to hear is "*I want greater security*".

Companies like this believe that without a basic pay you will have no choice but to perform. Their instinct will be to distrust your motives for wanting more security. And they will like the fact that the risk to them is minimal if they stick with a commission-only pay model.

6/ Ad-hoc / discretionary increases

This is by far the easiest pay structure for you to negotiate within. In fact describing it as a structure at all is a bit of a stretch. There are no formal rules here other than knowing who you have to ask.

That doesn't mean it's a complete free-for-all, though. Or that no thought at all is going to be put into staff salary levels. It just means that it presents fewer hurdles or timing issues than any other setup.

Opportunity Alert:

Even companies with rigid pay structures will make the odd exception if they value you highly enough

One of the things I said earlier is that for the right person in the right role the normal rules aren't going to apply. If you are perceived as being particularly valuable to a company (for whatever reason) then they will often go out of their way to try to find a way to accommodate you.

The key word here is "exception". Your role, or the skills that you bring, need to be unique or highly specialist and difficult to hire for. And important to the aspirations of the business.

So an excellent career goal is to get yourself into one of these specialist roles. And see what it does to your earning potential.

Or do what I have done more than once and actually **engineer a unique position for yourself** at your current employer.

Good to know: a company may use several or all of these different pay structures across the business

Chapter 6

WHAT SALARY SHOULD YOUR EMPLOYER BE PAYING YOU?

Don't forget to add the value of your 'special sauce' to the going rate for the role

===

I introduced the going rate as a concept way back in the first chapter. As a leader, I've always used the same philosophy when deciding how much to pay members of my team: **they would be paid the going rate for the role.**

I made the decision early on to be completely open with my team members about my commitment to that principle. That way everyone knew exactly where they stood and what any discussion with me around pay was going to centre on.

I would explain that, whilst I wouldn't be overpaying anyone, I knew how demotivating it was when you don't feel you are being paid fairly for your work. I wasn't going to let that happen.

To me, any alternative to paying the going rate would mean that one of us would always have an issue. Regardless of how that issue manifested itself, the impact was bound to be a negative effect on the team's performance.

As a result we rarely had any arguments over salaries. Our HR department couldn't argue with it. Our CEO couldn't argue with it. Our FD couldn't argue with it. My team couldn't argue with it. Because it's fair. It's consistent and it makes sense.

As you might expect, I took the same approach whenever I negotiated my own salary. And this is exactly the approach I am now recommending to you.

The question for you is, do you know what the current going rate is for your role and contribution right now?

Working out the fair "going rate" for yourself

Whenever people come to me for my advice on pay rises I ask them the following question: "*What made you choose the figure that you are planning on asking for?*"

More often than not this is where things start to get a little sketchy. The sort of responses I typically hear are:

- "*I've been here a while now and I think it's about time...*"

- "*Steve (in another dept) told me he earns that much and...*"

- "*It's what I need to earn to be able to afford to...*"

- "*I used to earn this at my last company...*" (when I was doing something totally different)

None of these are good reasons and this is why: they don't give me any sense that your value to the business has increased. Or that the amount you are asking for is in any way related to the contribution you are making to the company's profits.

They may well represent your motivation for wanting more money. But they are not a justification for the amount you are asking for. At least, not one that your employer is going to care about. Even if I sympathise with your position, I am going to struggle to say "yes" on the basis of one of the above examples.

Put it this way, plucking a figure from the air isn't credible and it won't sound credible to your boss. What you need instead is hard evidence. Hard evidence that relates to you, the role that you perform and what your specific contribution is right now. We'll look at how to get that evidence next.

Start by spending an hour researching salaries

The great thing about going rates is that, for most jobs, they are easy to research. The quickest method is probably to head to an online job site and look for any similar roles being advertised. Try to find positions that have been posted by similar sized companies in similar industries and locations. Leave your ego at the door and be honest with yourself when making your picks.

For example, is the job that you saw that's offering 30% more than your current salary really a fair comparison? Or does it just have the same job title? Look at the skills and experience that they are asking for and compare the responsibilities the role entails.

To make sure it really is a fair comparison use this checklist:

- Is the company a similar size to your current employer?

- Is the company in a comparable industry?

- Is the company in a comparable part of the country? (*London pay is higher, for example*)

- Are the responsibilities of that role the same as or very close to yours?

- Do you possess similar experience and qualifications to those they are looking for?

- Would you be in with a shot at that job if you had an interview?

If you can honestly answer yes to all of them then perfect, you can justify comparing the salary to yours

Your research is going to give you three important things:

- ✔ A range of salaries you can use to work out a representative "going rate" figure for your role
- ✔ Hard evidence of where that figure came from and why it is relevant and credible
- ✔ A handy reminder that there are other companies out there you could be working for, should you want to

Now add your 'special sauce' to the mix

We all have a special sauce. Made up of all the extra things we do, the personality and experience we bring and the positive impact we have on those around us. Some sauces are more valuable than others. But we do all have one. It's what makes us unique.

Taking on more than our job description becomes almost inevitable over time. It's called scope creep. The business and the needs of those around us change and we respond accordingly.

Many of us take on extra responsibilities or perform new tasks that either no-one else can or is willing to do. Or maybe you are simply the "best", the most productive, the one who deals with the difficult clients and turns them around.

Whatever it is that makes you special, try and put a genuine ££ value on the extra contribution you provide. As you are doing that, think about the impact you are having and what would happen if you suddenly stopped providing all these extras.

The acid test is this: could your boss get someone else in the company to do this additional work to the same standard without paying them extra to do it? And would they have to if you left?

What if I discover the salary I'm on now is fair?

Honestly, it can be a bit of a sobering slap in the face when this happens. How do you justify a big pay rise if you are already being paid the going rate for what you do?

The obvious answer to that question is probably giving you a sinking feeling right about now. But there are still upsides to discovering this reality:

- ✔ You can be comfortable that you are being paid fairly for the role. No-one is undervaluing you or ripping you off

- ✔ Your company appears committed to paying the going rate to their staff

- ✔ You now know that you need to focus on yourself if you want to be paid a higher salary

This last point is a much bigger win than you might imagine. Because you have probably been burning up a chunk of precious mental energy resenting your job up to this point. Blaming your employer for being greedy or your boss for not supporting you.

And it turns out that this isn't the case. Which means you can now direct all that mental power in a much more positive direction. Developing your skills to take on a role that will pay you the salary you desire.

If you don't know where to start with this then you could do far worse than asking your boss for their advice. The more active a role they play in your development, the more supportive they will be in the future when you are ready to step up.

Chapter 7

BUT WHAT SALARY SHOULD YOU ACTUALLY ASK FOR?

Your research has probably shown you a range. Time to pick a clear target to aim for

===

By now you should have developed a reasonable feel for the range of salaries that other companies are prepared to pay for someone doing your role. And you have the evidence to back this up.

Where exactly you belong within that range is going to be open to debate with your boss. To own that debate you now need to choose a specific figure that you will feel confident asking for.

These questions will help you to do that:

- Are you relatively new to your role or do you have many years' experience?

- Does your role require you to use specialist equipment, software or processes?

- Are you an absolute genius at what you do or simply very competent?

- Are you the go-to person for anything that's difficult?

- In your company is your role critical to their uniqueness in the market?

- What's the value to your employer of the extra contribution that you alone provide?

- If you left tomorrow, how long do you think it would take your manager to replace you completely?

How much higher is your target salary?

One or two thousand £ more than your current salary?
If so, I would actually suggest asking for a bit more than this, whilst promising not to ask again for a while

This does depend on how much your pay is now. If you are on a lower wage, or doing part-time work, then this amount may mean a significant increase to you. In which case it could be your sweet spot. But if you are already earning comfortably more than the minimum wage, or you are rapidly developing in your career, then I would be tempted to aim a little higher.

The reason being, it's a tiny amount for most companies to find and they may wonder why you are bothering them with it. Empathy-gap, I know.

Plus your boss will want to be sure that a pay rise of this size is going to be a genuine motivator for you. Both to stay with the company and to keep on doing great work.

I guess the key question is, would an extra £100 a month in your pocket make a noticeable difference to your lifestyle? If it would, or if this is more about principle than anything, then great.

Three to ten thousand £ more than your current salary?
For most people this is going to be the sweet spot for an ad-hoc raise, provided it is justified by your research

This amount is both big enough for you to notice and big enough for the company to see it as worth your making a fuss about. It's also still small enough (in company terms) for most businesses to be able to afford to swallow it without really noticing.

Tens of thousands £ more than your current salary?

This kind of increase will get noticed by more people, making your wider relationships that much more important

The higher your salary and the more senior your role, the easier it is to ask for a big pay rise. And if you are that lucky person who is already on a six figure salary then tens of thousands may only represent a 10% increase.

But if you are aiming for an increase of 20% or more, then even if it is fully justified it is going to raise a few eyebrows. Your boss will know this as well as anyone. They aren't going to put their neck on the line without being certain they won't get burned. So you want to make sure that you have a good relationship with all the key players who could influence or block your boss's decision.

Ironically, one question you should be ready for when asking for such a big pay rise is: *"why haven't you said anything about your salary before?"*

Three important rules of thumb

When making your decisions about how much more to ask for, keep these three thoughts in mind:

- ✔ It's better to negotiate one big increase now, rather than trying to negotiate several smaller increases over time

- ✔ The more unique your role is and the more critical your contribution, the more freedom you have to push your luck when it comes to asking for more money

- ✔ Your figure still has to be realistic, which means close enough to the going rate revealed by your research

Negotiating forward is a good option if your career is developing rapidly

Sometimes in your career you have periods where you really hit your stride at a company. You're making a real difference that everyone can see and you are still on a rapid improvement curve.

This is both exciting for you and great news for your employer. For they know that they have discovered a rising star. You are accelerating past more of your colleagues as every new day passes. And naturally you'd like rewarding for it. Again, please.

A surprising problem can occur when your own development is happening so quickly that the company's processes can't keep up

Say you are taking big strides in your development every few months. In your head, every time you've taken such a leap you feel your pay should rise accordingly. The going rate principle agrees with you.

But constantly spending precious time negotiating salaries with you simply isn't practical for most companies. Even if you are an exceptional talent, sooner or later you will come across as a pain if you just keep asking for pay rise after pay rise.

This is where negotiating forward comes in

You and your boss both want the same thing: your continued motivated development. Ideally without all the distractions and frustrations of constantly stressing and negotiating over pay.

What negotiating forward means is that you agree on your next pay rise (or rises) at the same time as negotiating this one. You get the benefit of having a clear target to focus on, together with certainty on what you will earn when you reach it. And it makes it clear to your boss that you have the motivation to keep excelling.

How do you go about negotiating forward?

If you recognise yourself as being in this situation then you have probably developed a reputation already for being bright, proactive and creative. So your introducing this concept to your manager won't seem out of character. It may even add further to your reputation for coming up with clever solutions.

Assuming your conversation around your pay rise has gone well and your boss has agreed to raise your salary, try something along the lines of this:

> "*I don't want to have to keep coming back to you every few months as I develop. So can we talk about how my salary would increase again if I keep improving and sort out some clear targets now?*"

Food for thought:

A higher salary isn't the only option you have when looking to increase the compensation you receive

It's easy for us to get fixated with salaries but why not consider the whole package that you receive from your employer in return for the work that you do for them?

It depends on the company, but there is often more flexibility around the additional benefits you receive than you might imagine. So if money isn't your main driver or if a restricted payroll budget is getting in the way of your pay rise, you could try getting creative.

Some wider package benefits to consider negotiating for:

- ✔ Increased company pension contributions
- ✔ More paid time off
- ✔ Shorter working days
- ✔ Volunteering days
- ✔ Free healthcare / life assurance
- ✔ Training courses paid for in company time
- ✔ Travel allowance
- ✔ Flexible or remote working

These options may be quite appealing to your boss as they would typically bypass a salary budget restriction. Your employer may also take the view that, by giving you benefits that mean something special to you personally, it would make it less likely for you to leave the business.

Some companies may baulk at the idea, but the reality is that they often cost less money to provide than it would cost them to pay you a higher salary. As well as being more effective if you end up feeling a bigger benefit in terms of your wellbeing.

Just be sure to do some research first if you are considering trying for any of these options. You need to make your own value judgement as to what each is "worth" to you when compared to getting a raise. And only you can answer that.

Chapter 8

ANCHORING, A KEY TOOL TO USE IN YOUR NEGOTIATION

Your range becomes a powerful weapon when you introduce the magic of anchoring

===

This is going to sound a little technical at first glance but I promise you it is really simple to do in practice. For what I am introducing here, if you aren't already aware of it, is an easy-to-use psychological principle. A principle called **anchoring**.

And it is going to make your salary negotiation a whole lot easier.

> **What is anchoring?**
>
> The anchoring effect is the principle that people tend to unconsciously latch onto the first number they hear when having to make a numbers-based value judgement. They then base their subsequent decision-making on that number.
>
> *Regardless of whether the number is accurate or even relevant to the topic*
>
> This first number is called the **anchor point**.

We are all hard-wired to make comparisons

Prices in shops are a prime example of this. How do we know if a supposed special offer is a rip-off or the bargain of the century? Simple. We look for something we already understand to compare it with. For example, the price in Lidl vs the price in Tesco.

If the price of our regular purchase is already in our head then that's where we are anchored. The special offer will either look cheap, not so special, or more expensive. Like I said, simple.

Simple, yes, but not infallible.

As psychologists and salespeople know, our anchors are remarkably easy to manipulate

There is a reason why most countries have rules around the use of anchors in retail promotions. They are so easy to exploit and so effective that it's important they are applied honestly.

Just before we get into using anchors to position your pay rise with your boss, I want to show you a famous textbook example of their power to influence our decision-making.

The anchoring effect: can your social security number influence how much you bid at an auction?

In 2006 a trio of economists named Dan Ariely, George Loewenstein and Drazen Prelec set up an experiment to answer this very question.

Their plan was to ask students at Massachusetts Institute of Technology to bid on a selection of different auction items. How much they bid was entirely up to each student. The students were told that they should choose their bids based solely on what they thought the item they were bidding on was really worth.

Just before the students started bidding they were each told to write down the last two digits of their social security number. And then to put a $ sign in front of it.

Unknown to the students, this figure would act as their anchor point. When the results of the auction came back the impact of this anchoring was remarkably consistent to see, whilst at the same time seeming to defy normal logic.

Just writing down their own social security number before they started bidding was all it took. It totally disrupted the students' ability to subsequently judge the value of the item they were bidding on. And it did so in a very specific way. The higher the number the student wrote down first, the higher the value they would place on the items they were buying.

For example, the students whose last two digits were highest (ranging from 80 to 99) bid an average of $26 for a trackball*.

Whilst the students whose last two digits were lowest (from 00 to 19) went on to bid an average of just $9 for the very same item.

This pattern was repeated throughout the research, regardless of what item was being bid on, or its true value.

*A trackball was a popular alternative to a computer mouse at the time, in case you were wondering

How to set the right anchor points to use with your boss

Actually, before we do that let's cover off why understanding anchor points is worth the effort. You see, this is all to do with our universal instinct to always want a bargain. To not feel like we are paying more than we have to for something.

You basically want your boss to instinctively feel that your request is fair. And anchoring is a great tool to help us to do that.

What if we didn't bother providing our own anchor point?

That's easy. Your boss would simply choose an anchor of their own. They would look for a handy comparison figure that they already have available to them. Which would most likely be your current salary.

As a comparison to your current salary, any request you make for a higher wage is going to look expensive. So we are going to introduce our own anchors to change their perspective. And anchors work even better when you combine them with ranges.

A range anchors you in two places

You are probably ahead of me by now but the great thing about a range of figures is that it anchors you at both ends. You see the high figure and the low figure and automatically set them in your mind as the maximum and minimum amounts to consider.

Instinctively, then, for it to feel comfortable, any value you are going to accept as being "right" has to be somewhere in the middle of the two. Your brain is set up to expect it.

The range we are going to be using is the one you created from your salary research. Your "going rate" range in other words. Introduced in the right way, your boss's instinct will be to consider that a fair salary figure should sit somewhere within that range.

There are two important things you have to understand in order for the combined power of anchoring and ranges to have the greatest effect.

The first is that the order in which you introduce your two anchors matters. In this case, the highest and lowest salaries from your rescarched "going rate" range.

The second is that the salary that you are actually asking for needs to sit in the lower half of your range.

1/ With a range, your boss will be mainly focused on the first of the two salary figures they hear

Even though a range gives you two anchor points, it is still the first one that has the most power. For your pay rise conversation, you want that number to be the higher of your two figures.

Let's say your "going rate" research suggests a range of salaries from £30,000 to £38,000. If that was the order you introduced them to your boss, then the first number they would hear would be the lower figure of £30,000. And that's the figure they would compare to what you then went on to ask for.

That's better than their comparing it to your current salary, assuming your current salary is below the range minimum (see below for a tip to make sure this is the case).

But your best option is this: Swap the order around and start from the top. Tell your boss that the "going rate" ranges from £38,000 down to £30,000.

That way, when your boss registers the numbers, their main anchor point will be the higher figure of £38,000 (with the lower anchor point also uncomfortably higher than your current salary if you have chosen your range well),

Remember: if you want your desired salary to seem more like a bargain, introduce the higher anchor point first.

2/ Our comfort zone when it comes to judging value will always be in the lower half of a range

This comes back once more to our universal desire for a bargain. Which in itself is really just another aspect of our natural competitive instinct. We all like to win.

Your boss will know logically that the new salary you are asking for is an increase over your current pay. By introducing a range to provide two anchor points, though, we have moved their focus away from your current salary. They are now focused instead on the top and bottom of the range you have provided.

As long as the salary you are looking for is nearer the lower end of this range it is going to feel more emotionally comfortable to them. This doesn't suddenly make your pay rise a slam dunk. But, as long as your research has been realistic, it does remove a key defensive barrier. One less hurdle for you to worry about.

Caution: you may now have to adjust your range

This is going to feel a little like cheating but, as the two points above make clear, your "going rate" range is more than just supporting evidence. It is a powerful psychological tool that you need to make sure is working in your favour.

And the truth is, you are just being selective in which examples you choose to show your boss. It's your research, after all.

The two things you need to make sure of are:

- ✔ The lower end of your range should be higher than your current salary
- ✔ The new salary you will be asking for should be in the lower half of your range

BECAUSE I'M WORTH IT

Happily, if you need to adjust your range it is easy to do. You are simply going to choose which examples you are going to share with your boss in order to move the ends of the range up or down.

To raise the lower end of the range
You can simply drop the lowest paying example jobs that you found

To raise the top end of the range
Do some more research to see if you can find a higher paying example job to introduce

Even if that means being a bit cheeky and using an example that isn't directly comparable to your current role. That's the beauty of how anchoring works. An unrepresentative example is still going to be effective, as long as you are honest about it.

For example, you could say to your boss:

"The going rate seems to range from £44,000 down to £30,000. Though, to be honest, I think the £44,000 example I saw was pretty specialist so I'm not going to share the details of that one with you"

You have still effectively anchored your boss to the £44,000 to £30,000 range. Perfect if the fair going rate figure you are targeting happens to be around the £35,000 mark.

Chapter 9

TIMING IS EVERYTHING

You definitely deserve a raise and now you can prove it. But is this a good time to ask?

===

Comedians, sportspeople and chefs all know the importance of getting your timing right. And when it comes to asking for your pay rise it's not just a matter of how ready *you* are. You need to be confident that the right conditions are in place before you act.

Like going to the beach on a sunny day or booking a skiing trip in winter. There are good times to choose to ask for a pay rise. And by the same token there are times to avoid at all costs.

Imagine yourself in this situation at work:

- You're feeling really confident about your value to the company and you believe that you deserve a pay rise
- Your research clearly backs up the new salary you are after
- You've been walking the walk for months
- Your boss has been praising your contribution
- Just 6 weeks ago the company gave everyone a small annual pay rise saying it was all they could afford
- Your boss doesn't seem their normal self and is cutting back on any projects that cost money
- New business has gone a bit quiet; the usual buzz in sales is missing

What are the general vibes you are getting?

Does it sound like everything is rosy in the garden or do you get the impression that times are tight?

It can be frustrating to wait, but sometimes waiting is the best thing you can do. Because the conditions have to be right for you to get what you want. Even if your boss desperately wants to give you a raise, they may not be in a position to be able to. Something I have experienced myself in the past.

How to choose your perfect moment

Your ideal moment is the point at which your boss is at their most receptive. With the company itself being in a good financial position to be able to afford it.

This is what that looks like:

- ✔ You are in your boss's good books
  (*consistently high performing*)

- ✔ The company is obviously doing well
  (*good sales and positive vibes*)

- ✔ Any "normal" pay rise date is months away
  (*in either direction*)

- ✔ Your boss seems to be in a happy place
  (*not stressed or preoccupied*)

You can normally feel the mood in a business. When things are going well there is a buzz and senior managers are relaxed.

It gets even better if the company is growing rapidly and sales are flying. Because you can normally be a lot cheekier with your pay request and get away with it.

What if you're stuck in a "bad time to ask" with no sign of it ending?

Then sooner or later you are going to want to have a conversation with your boss about the state of the business.

Let them know that your salary is becoming an issue for you and that you haven't raised it until now because of the obvious problems the company is having. That you are getting concerned about how serious things might be and you would like their view on the situation.

If they convince you that things are going to improve and that any problems aren't terminal then here's your opportunity to bring your pay rise up. Say that you understand what they are saying and that as soon as things start to pick up you would like a salary conversation with them please.

Chapter 10

THE WEEK BEFORE YOUR MEETING

Time to get all your ducks in a row, finish your prep, and check for last minute issues

===

In the chapter on timing I mentioned choosing a sunny day to go to the beach. Let's continue with that analogy to remind ourselves why preparation is so important when we want to make sure that things are going to go well.

Let's imagine our trip to the beach is with a close friend who we haven't seen in a while. You want it to be a really special day out for the both of you. You have two options to make sure you have the day you want:

Option A/ Just wing it on the day

You jump in the car, head roughly towards the coast and hope for the best. It's fun to do it this way. Exciting, even. Minimal effort required and it may work out just fine.

Or you may end up getting lost. It's raining at the coast. There's nowhere to park. Everything's shut as it's out of season.

Option B/ You spend a bit of time preparing beforehand

You started by choosing a beach where it was forecast to be sunny all day. Then you planned a route and where to park, having Googled the traffic before setting off.

TripAdvisor has suggested things to do, places to eat and drink, and confirmed that everything that matters is open. You've even booked lunch to be on the safe side.

As you set off, having checked you've got your shades and phone, you are confident this is going to be a great day.

Sure, you may have been fine just jumping in the car. And it would definitely have been less effort. But by doing a little work beforehand you can be confident everything is likely to go to plan.

What final preparation should you be doing?

With all these completed you will be in a confident frame of mind to book your meeting with your boss:

- ✔ Give your boss some great work a few days before you book your meeting in

- ✔ Have a few positive chats with any key players (or members of their team) to keep you fresh in their minds

- ✔ Get a feel for how well your team is performing overall

- ✔ Check when your boss has some free slots in their diary

- ✔ Check if any key players are going on leave, in case they are needed

- ✔ Sound out colleagues for how well the company is doing

- ✔ Practise what you are going to say (but don't try and learn a rigid script)

- ✔ Know what your research says and print it out to bring along with you

You are now well prepared to discuss any points that your boss may bring up when you meet.

Booking the meeting with your boss

This is another timing matter. Because believe it or not, even the time of day that you have your meeting is going to make a difference. The reason is something called "decision fatigue".

How decision fatigue affects your boss

Being a decision-maker can be great for the ego but it does use up a lot of mental energy. So as the day goes on and the problems keep coming at them your boss is going to start to get tired.

As they tire, their concentration suffers. Battling this then uses up more of their mental energy and so they tire some more.

Their mood slowly worsens as the day continues. They start to get irritable. Their decisions becoming less and less considered. More than anything they need to take a refreshing break.

And then in you walk with your important question and a load of research to share with them. The perfect moment to have your meeting?

Work out the times of day that your boss is at their best

For most busy managers in 9-5 roles, decision fatigue starts to set in late-morning. Then there is some recovery time over lunch before it sets in again mid-afternoon.

In other roles and environments it will be different. When their day starts, whether they are an introvert or an extrovert, their eating habits and various other factors will all have an influence.

Just look out for patterns of behaviour such as when your boss is at their chattiest. When they seem cheerful and energetic. Try to book your meeting for the time of day when your boss is normally at their freshest.

How should you describe this meeting to your boss?

My advice is to keep it simple and confidently tell your boss what the meeting is about when you book it. Try to be as relaxed and matter-of-fact as you can, remembering to wear a smile as you talk.

Introducing it so positively sets the scene for your boss to be more positive in return. This is because we tend to mirror the behaviour we are seeing in others.

It really can be as simple as saying: *"I'd like to talk about my salary with you - can I book a meeting with you next week?"*

One of the benefits of booking ahead is that it gives your boss plenty of time to prepare and potentially to be in a better position to say *"yes"* on the day. It also allows them the opportunity to talk to the other key players first to get their thoughts.

Crucially, it ensures your boss will feel in control of the situation. Not facing an ambush. The more in control they feel, the more relaxed they are going to be. And the more relaxed they are, the greater your chance of getting the answer that you want.

But do be prepared in case your boss wants to discuss it there and then

This is the thing about your boss being in control. Some managers, and particularly business owners, like to tackle things head-on.

This could be a good sign so be ready with your evidence and your pitch just in case. Or you can simply smile and say you'd prefer to come properly prepared, if that's ok with them.

If they do insist, then don't get flustered. Show them your confidence and follow the steps in the next chapter.

The night before your meeting

Your boss is going to pick up on how calm, confident and fresh you are during your meeting. These are important sensory clues that influence emotional decision-making at a subconscious level. Their gut will be telling them if they can trust the decisions that their head is consciously making.

This means the night before your meeting is going to be especially important. It's the time to get everything you need together before relaxing and getting a good night's sleep. This isn't the time to go out partying.

Don't imagine the next day over and over in your head, either. If your mind tries that game then just listen to the things it throws at you without engaging with them. You'll be surprised how quickly your mind gets bored and gives up. You can't predict the future so don't try.

- ✔ Eat a nice meal that you know won't upset your stomach or leave you feeling bloated

- ✔ Check you have everything you need placed in your bag (pen, paper, research etc.)

- ✔ Sort out what you are going to wear and have it ready

- ✔ Set the alarm a little earlier than usual to give yourself plenty of time in the morning

- ✔ Go to bed early, nicely hydrated

Chapter 11

SHOW TIME: THE DAY YOU ASK YOUR BOSS FOR A PAY RISE

The big day has arrived. You're prepared and feeling confident. Let's make it count

===

Before we get to the meeting itself, please read this:

I want you to think about this section a little differently in terms of how you put it into practice. This is because you have to treat your meeting with your boss as a natural conversation between two people. You can only control what one of you is going to say and that person has to sound and act just like you at all times. So **always** use your own words and natural style and be ready to improvise and calmly respond to any curveballs that your boss might throw at you.

The reason I am highlighting this now is because I will be taking you through a planned conversation in order to explain my recommended approach to you. Even though you can't actually predict how a conversation is going to go, because you don't know what the other person is going to say.

The reason for planning things out beforehand is just so you get everything nice and clear in your head. Something that is also going to help you with your confidence during the meeting.

So please take some inspiration from this section. Understand all the principles behind it and digest the example conversations.

But remember this is a guide, not a script

Always be yourself

Something to be aware of is this: your boss will have already decided their starting position

Before you even start talking, your boss will have planned in their heads to do one of these 3 things:

1. Give you a pay rise
   (*and probably has a figure in mind*)

2. Not give you a pay rise
   (*and has their reason ready*)

3. Go in with an open mind
   (*and they will see what your pitch is*)

They are still going to listen to what you have to say out of politeness and respect for you. But, having given them notice about the subject of your meeting, their mindset will already be in one of these three places.

The important thing to realise is that **you can still influence them in this meeting** to change their mind. That includes the potential to talk your manager out of giving you a pay rise if you are not careful. Even if they were convinced before the meeting that they were going to say yes to your request.

This is why it is essential for you to go about your meeting in the right way. The nicer you are. The better your attitude. The more you show your appreciation for them. These are all things that will influence your boss to feel compelled to give you something back in return.

Even if their original mindset wasn't in the place you might have hoped it would be.

1/ Start off with the niceties

This is your meeting so the onus is on you to run things and to set the general tone. You want to make sure that your boss feels in full control of their decision. But remember that the meeting itself is in your hands. The tone you are looking to set is one that is relaxed, positive and collaborative.

A good way to warm things up is this:

- ✔ Nice warm smile
- ✔ Check this is still a good time for them
- ✔ Thank your boss for taking the time to talk to you when you know they are are busy
- ✔ Open with a bit of small talk. Maybe ask about their family. If you know they are working on a big project or have just moved house then ask them how it's going
- ✔ Chat about the things you normally discuss. The more positive the subject, the better. This is all about putting your boss in a relaxed state of mind

Then, when the moment feels natural, move on to telling them why you wanted to have this conversation.

2/ Tell your boss why you wanted to have this conversation

I said earlier that your actions would speak louder than your words. Which meant proving your additional worth to your boss before you asked for this meeting. And demonstrating all the qualities you were going to use to support your case.

Assuming this is what you have been doing, now is the time to remind them just what a great asset you are. You can use your introduction to talk about the contribution you are making. How you think it has increased and the impact this is having.

Give them a few examples and ask if they've noticed. As you talk, start weaving these examples together as evidence of your capability and any big steps you have made.

As much as possible you want to seek reassurance from your boss that you are doing the right things. Things that they would like to see more of from you.

Seeking reassurance is helpful for these two reasons:

- ✔ It gives you an early indicator of how realistic you are being in your self-assessment of your value

- ✔ You are getting your boss used to agreeing with you

For why that second point matters psychologically, I'm going to introduce you to the "saying yes" trick

The "saying yes" trick (*note: it comes with a "but"*)

This is more simple and effective psychology, one that is often mis-used as a blunt instrument by sales teams.

Basically, as people we like to find common ground. We are drawn to others who we find ourselves agreeing with.

Here's how the principle works:

- ✔ You ask a question that the other person is very likely to agree with

- ✔ And you keep on doing this (*preferably with questions that are relevant to the ultimate topic*)

- ✔ Until you finally reach the question you really wanted to ask

- ✔ Having agreed with you so far, the other person is now more likely to agree with this point too

That's the theory, and when you use it subtly it can be really effective.

Here comes the "*but*"

However, it can backfire horribly if the other person feels they are being manipulated. If they notice you doing it (*"do you like getting a bargain?", "do you agree that water is wet?"*) then up come the defences.

Remember what I said about your boss needing to feel in control? If you try to railroad your boss into literally saying "yes" to things, expect it to end badly.

What you are looking for instead is general consistent agreement with the points you are making. Not robotically asking a bunch of loaded questions to generate a single-word "yes" response. It's a conversation, after all.

Why you should give your boss something to say "no" to as well

Chris Voss, former FBI hostage negotiator, emphasises the importance of prompting the right kind of *"no"* in his excellent book *"Never split the difference"*. Chris explains that being able to say *"no"* is a key factor in making the person you are negotiating with feel safe, secure and in control of the situation.

And you do want your boss to feel they are in control.

One method you could try is this: in one of the examples where you are explaining your greater impact, say to your boss *"I wasn't sure if you wanted me to stop doing this?"*

Their saying *"no"* here would absolutely be the right answer for you. It leaves them feeling in control, whilst still agreeing that you are doing the right thing.

Tip: why not try this little trick out in other situations beforehand as a bit of practice?

What if... your boss isn't agreeing with you as you were expecting?

Firstly, don't panic if you are getting the odd "no" vibes when you were expecting a "yes" response. This was always going to be an open conversation so you have to treat it as such.

If this does happen, ask your boss some open questions to get a bit more clarity on where they are coming from. An open question is one that won't prompt a simple yes or no answer - think in terms of what, how, where etc. If you think they are being reasonable then you just need to take it on the chin and move on.

Or you could try getting a bit more specific with your question to see if you can get back to a "yes". For example, if your boss disagreed that your whole team was working better, you could say: *"I think Tina and Chris are working really well together, though - don't you agree?"*

But if your boss is disagreeing with nearly everything you say then you may need to have a rethink. In fact, it is probably a good idea for you to sense-check if it is worth continuing with your plan to ask for a pay rise today.

For example, by saying: *"I thought I was doing pretty well but maybe I've been kidding myself. How would you say I have been doing?"*

Then listen carefully to whatever your boss says next and take a view on where to go from there.

You can find more advice on this situation in the "What if... your boss didn't react as you hoped?" section on page 109

An example conversation:

Why you wanted this meeting

(always use your own words to sound natural)

<You>
"Shall we get started? Do you mind if I go first?"

<Your Boss>
"No, go ahead"

<You>
"Perfect. Before I talk to you about the research I've been doing, I just wanted to sense-check that the effort I have been putting in recently has been going in the right direction and that it's adding genuine value."

"I think the work I have been doing to motivate the team has had a real impact. Have you seen any improvement?"

<Your Boss>
"I have, yes"
"Actually, it's been really noticeable"

<You>
"That's really good to hear. What have you noticed?"

<Your Boss>
"The whole team just seems to be in a better place. Happier."

\<You\>
"I wasn't sure if you wanted me to stop spending time on it?"

\<Your Boss\>
"No - quite the opposite. I think it is really beneficial"

\<You\>
"Great - I'll keep at it then"

"I'm also really proud of how the XYZ project went. You thought that would save around £10K per month - that's right, isn't it?"

\<Your Boss\>
"Yes, that sounds about right"

Once you have your boss agreeing with you over a few points, you can move on

\<You\>
"I'm so glad I wasn't kidding myself - and I just wanted to thank you for your support and help with my development so far. It really means a lot to me.

"I really feel that I have stepped up a level these past few months"

3/ Introducing your research

Assuming things have been going to plan so far, this is where you should be at:

- ✔ You started off by setting a friendly, relaxed and chatty tone for the conversation
- ✔ You have clearly demonstrated the great contribution you are making to the business
- ✔ Your boss has agreed that, yes, you are making a positive impact
- ✔ Your boss has been generally agreeing with your points throughout the conversation

And you have just thanked your boss for their support and help in your development.

Your next step is to introduce this logical principle:

As your contribution to the business has grown, you felt there was a good chance that the going rate for your role would now be higher too.

You wanted to find out what a fair salary would be for the level you are currently at in your role. And you thought that the best way for you to check this was to do some research into what others in the industry were being paid.

An example conversation:
Introducing your research
(always use your own words to sound natural)

\<You\>
"Something that matters a lot to me is that I always get paid fairly for the work that I do."

"And I know *\<company name\>* is generally committed to paying people the going rate."

"So I've been looking into what the going rate would be now for the work I am currently doing. Basically by doing a bit of research online into similar roles at similar companies."

"This is how I went about it…" *\<explain your process\>*

"…does that sound like a reasonable approach to you?"

\<Your Boss\>
"Yes, that makes sense to me"

4/ Take your boss through your research

This bit is basically a game of "show and tell". At this point your confidence really wants to be shining through. If you are hesitant about your examples then your boss may start to question if you are just trying it on by using them.

Come across as positive and relaxed about your examples, though, and they will both add credibility and clearly demonstrate the amount of thought that you have put into this. Having your visuals to hand will add even more weight to your pitch.

- If your meeting is face-to-face, remember to bring the printouts with you
- If your meeting is remote, then share your screen and show them screenshots

Start by telling them the the range you have identified

Remembering to put the higher figure first, as this is the main anchor point (page 68) you want your boss to register.

For example:

"What I have found is that the going rate seems to range from around £YY,000 down to £XX,000"

"The lower figure seems to be for people who <give a brief description of the jobs at that level, based on your research>*"*

"The higher figure is more for people who <give a brief description of the jobs at that level, based on your research>*"*

Now talk your boss through some of your examples

Don't be afraid to say that you know they won't all be directly comparable. Especially the one at the very top end of the salaries.

But do say that these are the closest examples you could find. And that you are confident that your role would fit somewhere within that range.

At this point, it is a good idea to sense-check what your boss is thinking

The easiest way being to simply ask them straight. Don't be surprised if they say that your examples aren't directly equivalent. Especially the ones with the biggest salaries.

As long as you trust your research you should stick to your guns. You don't want to get into any kind of argument. Just calmly and confidently explain again why you believe they are relevant to working out the salary you should be on.

The more relaxed and positive you come across at this point the better.

Remember:

Right now, your boss just needs to entertain the idea that your role may lie somewhere within this range of salaries

5/ Tell your boss what you think your salary should be now

This is the big moment you have been building up to. I know I keep saying it, but it is really important that you stay calm, confident and relaxed as you talk.

Your positivity and confidence are the things that will force your boss to take the number you are about to tell them seriously. To understand that you are genuine in your belief that this would be a fair salary to pay you. That you aren't just aiming for the stars.

And your calm, smiling demeanour is going to reassure them that they can take their time and think. Which they are probably going to need to do.

If everything is going well so far then this part should just flow naturally

So all that's left for you to do is tell your boss where you sit in that range and why. Keep it matter-of-fact and do everything you can to avoid seeming confrontational.

Your salary pitch should come across as a perfectly reasonable thing for them to agree with:

"Where I think I sit in the range is around here, at the £ZZ,000 mark, because: <describe your role/competence/company/location characteristics, compared to the role examples you are using>"

If your suggested new salary is quite a leap

You may want to acknowledge this as a potential objection by quickly adding:

"I know this is quite an increase and it was a surprise to me too, but this looks to be the general going rate for what I am now doing."

6/ The "what do you think?" moment

Just before you pause for breath you have one last question to ask:

"So... what do you think?"

And that's it. You have completed the hard part and now you are handing the baton back to your boss.

Now it's your boss's turn to lead. And you should let them

If your boss has heard you out this far then it is clear that they both respect and value you. They have given you their time and they have listened to your reasoning.

You now need to give them exactly the same respect back. So listen carefully to their response and **don't interrupt them.**

Try to avoid the mistake of listening with the intent to reply as you will miss important information if you do this. Instead, listen with the intent of learning and understanding. Stay calm and wait for your boss to either finish or to ask you a question.

If your boss appears to be thinking, remain quiet. Your silence can be a surprisingly powerful tool here.

But do expect your conversation to continue

A lot of people get past the "ta-daa!" moment of their big question and then expect to receive an instant "yes" or "no". In reality this isn't very likely, unless you push it. Which probably won't do you any favours.

Your boss will need time to digest things. So keep being positive and honest with your answers. The more maturely you handle this part, the more professionally you will come across.

7/ Your boss is making positive noises

This is obviously exactly what we are hoping for. So if your boss is basically agreeing with you at this point then well done. That really is fantastic news.

Remember, a positive response can be many things at this stage:

- "*I think you're right*"
- "*That seems fair*"
- a straight "*Yes, OK*"
- even "*I'll try*"

Any of these responses means that you have won your boss over.

Don't count your chickens just yet, though

Your manager may be on your side, but they will still have some work to do to make it all official.

For example, they may have to:

- Get your new salary agreed and signed off by their boss
- Discuss it with HR
- Run it past the Financial Director
- Sense-check the research you shared with them
- Consider any implications for the rest of their team

So smile while you thank your boss and tell them that you really appreciate it. Then ask them this question:

"*What happens now?*"

This will tell you your boss's next steps - and the timescale you can expect them to happen in.

After that you can leave the meeting feeling very proud of yourself. You took the initiative and had the confidence to ask for the pay rise you wanted. Now it looks like there is every chance you're going to get yourself the perfect result.

Chapter 12

FOLLOWING UP AFTER YOUR MEETING

You must keep any promises you made. Be sure to hold your boss to theirs as well

===

Until the day you see your increased salary appear in your payslip, your pay rise isn't real. Which is why it's so important to make sure any agreements that have been made are kept to.

What did you agree to do following your meeting?

If you agreed to do anything as part of the deal then you have one simple rule to follow: *whatever it was you said you were going to do, make sure you do it.*

This could include:

- Setting up any meetings you said you would organise
- Carrying out any extra research you were asked to do
- Completing any work or learning that was part of the deal
- Speaking to anyone you were supposed to get an agreement from

In short, you should see whatever you agreed to do as an integral part of the deal to get your pay rise.

That also goes for anything you agreed *not* to do. For example, if you were told not to discuss it with any of your colleagues. **I know at least one person who had their hard-earned pay rise swiftly reversed for ignoring that particular instruction.**

What about your boss - what did they agree to do?

As long as you keep your side of the bargain then you have the right to expect the same courtesy from your boss. So if they told you they were going to do something, you can feel perfectly entitled to politely hold them to it.

If possible, get your boss to agree to a specific timescale for each item they have committed to do. Then, as the deadlines approach, you can ask them gently how they are getting on.

If anything goes past an agreed date you should mention it. Be polite but do look disappointed whilst you say you understand that they are probably busy.

Then ask them when they think they can do it once more.

What if your boss keeps on stalling?

If your boss keeps giving you the brush-off then there could be a bigger issue at play. Maybe they are having trouble with one of the other key players. Try booking in another meeting with them to find out what the problem is.

There may be a clue in the list of drivers that we looked at on page 19. Your boss won't want to come across to you as being weak or not in control. They also don't want to lose one of their best staff members. So if there is a problem in the background they may be stalling to try to avoid any of those things happening.

If this does turn out to be the case then it is another opportunity for you to build your relationship with them. Handled well, it could make your boss more determined than ever to support you. So be understanding as you explain that you would really like to know the truth about any delay.

Don't worry, most pay rises are going to go through smoothly

The above points are all important to understand and to plan for, but they really are just in case. The majority of the time it's simply a matter of not letting anything silly trip you up at this final hurdle.

Most managers will know exactly what they can and can't commit to on the spot. Which means most promised pay rises are going to go through without any kind of hitch.

And when you do get your payslip and see that your salary has indeed gone up, there is one final task left for you to do:

Celebrate. You did it!

What If (1)…

YOUR BOSS DIDN'T REACT AS YOU HOPED?

A "yes" response isn't guaranteed but don't fret, you can still turn this into a positive

===

You've told your boss your figure and have just asked them the question: "*So... what do you think?*"

Right now you are listening carefully to your boss's response and doing your best not to interrupt them. And you don't like what you are hearing...

At this point you need to stay in control of your emotions and not start to get angry, upset or defensive if their answer isn't immediately positive. It really is important that you don't let your head drop or start to lose focus.

Instead, let's look at what your boss is really saying to you:

"It isn't a good time / the money isn't available"

Your boss didn't say that you don't deserve a pay rise. Let that sink in for just a moment. Because this may genuinely be a simple issue of timing.

My advice here would be:

Tell your boss "that's disappointing to hear" and say calmly that you do understand the situation

Ask your boss if they agree that your suggested figure would be fair if the budget were available. If they agree it would, ask them when a good time would be to revisit your pay rise. Then put that date in both your diaries to bring it up again.

Your boss thinks the salary you are suggesting is too high

This implies that they are happy with your research and your representative range of salaries. They just don't agree with your view on where you sit within it.

At this point you are actually halfway there. This is already a positive start. For what you are doing now is entering into a negotiation.

Your boss has entertained the idea that your salary should be higher. You are simply disagreeing over the amount.

My advice here would be:

Ask your boss where they think you sit in the scale and what it is that makes them think that

Listen carefully to their thought process and then choose from these options:

- If you are happy enough with their suggested figure then why not accept it?

- If you disagree with their reasoning try giving them a positive counterargument, remembering your preparation

- Or offer to go away and do some more salary research ready for a follow-up meeting

Whichever option you choose, reassure your boss that you just want to be paid a figure that you both agree is fair. One that reflects your contribution to the business and the going rate for what you are doing. And remember to thank them for agreeing that your salary should be looked at.

Your boss thinks that you are kidding yourself

This is going to be the hardest response for you to hear for obvious reasons. But it could also hold the key to your future development and career success. As long as you keep control of your emotions.

In this instance your boss has not only rejected the amount you have asked for. They have also rejected that you belong within the salary range that you so diligently researched.

Their reasons for doing this could include:

- You have very different views over the scope of your role and the contribution you are making

- They believe your salary research was flawed

- Your general performance, contribution or attitude are lacking somewhere in their eyes

Whatever reasoning they give you, you should listen carefully to them and take it all in. Then, having listened carefully, you need to ask yourself this question and answer it as honestly as you can: "*Could they be right?*"

There's no shame in it if you think they are. The only shame would be if you don't learn from it. Instead of feeling angry or embarrassed, you need to see this as a golden opportunity.

My advice here would be:

Take a moment to digest what your boss has told you and to gather your thoughts before thanking them

Now focus your mind on taking something positive away from the meeting. Ask your boss for their help in doing something about it.

If this has come as a genuine shock to you then maybe your boss finds it difficult generally to give you negative feedback. So hearing it now for the first time may stick in your throat a bit. But if you sense that your boss generally has your best interests at heart then you should thank them for their honesty and ask for their help in reaching your goals.

By doing this you play into at least two of their key drivers: being in control and feeling good about themselves. More importantly, you are building yourself a clear path to follow to secure a pay rise in the future.

If you do ask your boss for their help, you have to mean it sincerely:

- ✔ Listen carefully to what you need to do
- ✔ Write down any actions you need to take
- ✔ Put timescales against each point
- ✔ Put the necessary effort in to improve your skills
- ✔ Ask for regular feedback on your progress

It can be upsetting to realise that you aren't yet as capable as you had imagined. But it can also be the start of an amazing journey. You just need to recognise it for the opportunity it is; the opportunity to learn, to develop and to grow as a person. So embrace it and see where it takes you.

This approach also offers you another major benefit. When your manager commits to helping you with your development they will have a natural vested interest in your future success.

Which will be very useful when the time is right for you to try again for your pay rise.

Whatever happens, please be proud of yourself. You found the courage to ask the question

Your manager will have understood that this is a stressful subject for you to talk about. They will know how much your salary and sense of self-worth mean to you and that there may also be other pressures facing you in the background.

So they will have expected a degree of nervousness and won't be too surprised if your emotions are a little charged because of it. That's not a problem if they can give you the answer you wanted.

But if they can't, they will have been bracing for the worst when thinking about your reaction. This is why your staying calm and positive in the face of bad news has such a powerful effect.

By doing this you will almost certainly change the way your boss sees you. Just by asking for your pay rise in the right way and handling the conversation and their feedback so professionally.

No normal person enjoys giving bad news by the way. Career relationships should be seen as long-term so get this right and it will only help your relationship with your boss going forwards.

Of course, there is an alternative to staying where you are

Do you stick or twist? That's the other question you might want to think about. Your current employer is a known quantity and you have just been given a pretty good idea of what you need to do to increase your pay there in the future.

From your research you also have a pretty good idea of what you could be earning elsewhere. Did any of those roles seem tempting when you looked at them? Moving to another company is always a risk but then so is staying where you are. How do the two options make you feel now that you know where you stand in your current role? Is now a good time for you to roll the dice?

What If (2)…

THE GOING RATE FOR YOUR ROLE IS THE ONLY CHANGE?

This section is if your own development isn't your driver for wanting a higher salary

===

Nearly all of us have periods in our career where we do the same job for a while. Maybe because we love it, or maybe because we have found a natural level we are comfortable with for now.

This doesn't mean our pay shouldn't still increase over time. In fact you could be due a higher salary for all sorts of reasons:

- ✔ You have become super-efficient
  (*because you know the system inside out*)

- ✔ You are the go-to person for challenging situations
  (*because of your years of experience*)

- ✔ You have built a great external network
  (*because these relationships are valuable to the business*)

- ✔ The going rate for roles like yours have increased generally
  (*because these skills are in wider demand*)

- ✔ Salaries in general have increased
  (*because of inflation*)

Whatever the reason is, you can be confident that everything I have said in the book so far still stands. You can use the same approach and the same techniques to ask for your pay rise.

You just need to swap out talking about your development and the added contribution you are making. And replace it with the relevant reasoning that applies to you.

The most obvious change to make will be in your introduction to the meeting

In the section on page 91 titled *"Tell your boss why you wanted to have this conversation"* I was suggesting that you talk about your increased contribution and the impact you are having.

In your case, though, you should drop the "increased" and simply talk about the great contribution that you make. Talk about how much you enjoy working at the company and that you believe that you are doing a good job.

If there are any things you do that make your contribution a bit special then throw them in. For example, how you've "noticed that everyone seems to come to you for advice."

You can still use the "saying yes" trick (as explained on page 92) to get your boss to start agreeing with you.

The other thing that may need to change is how you ask for the right kind of "no" (page 93). Remember that you want your boss to feel in control of the situation. And that asking them a question where they can answer "no" (in a way that means a positive for you) is a great way of doing this.

For example:

"Do you think that Chris or Steve would have handled those situations as well as I did?"

BECAUSE I'M WORTH IT

What If (3)…

YOUR BOSS OWNS THE COMPANY?

Company owners see things differently to most managers. This is what to understand

===

The biggest difference to be aware of is on the emotional side. When your boss also owns the company you will find that questions to do with money quickly become personal to them.

The logic side of determining how big your salary should be, together with your general approach to having a pay rise conversation, remains exactly the same as for any other manager.

What will cloud things, though, is your boss's instinctive *emotional* reaction to being asked to increase your salary. Because it literally *is* their money that you are asking for.

Building a company from scratch is seriously hard work

It's not unusual to see an uncomfortable empathy gap between a business owner and their staff:

Disgruntled employees who imagine their boss enjoying a life of luxury, creaming off the profits that are being created for them.

Resentful business owners who see their staff as spoiled or lazy. Pampered by a company that pays them anyway regardless of whether the business made a profit that month.

I'm being unkind, I know. But I'm sure we've all experienced examples of the above attitudes. And realistically there will be an element of truth to each of them at times.

What this means in practice is that a degree of entitlement can occasionally embed itself in the business-owner mindset. It may help you to understand where this mindset comes from and why.

Your business-owner boss will probably have:

- Worked ridiculously long hours for many years, probably for little or no reward at times
- Taken big personal financial risks with no guarantees or safety net in place
- Made huge personal sacrifices, including time with their family and friends
- Put themselves under enormous stress over long periods
- Wondered many times "*is it really worth all this effort?*"

They can forget at times that comparing their position as a business owner to yours as an employee is comparing apples and pears. The two situations and what they offer in terms of risk and reward are totally different.

A business-owner boss with this mindset can start feeling that your getting paid more equates directly with their getting paid less. Particularly if business isn't going as well as they would like.

So they need careful handling if you are going to get past:

- Their ego, with no-one above them to worry about
- Their view that you are in a privileged position in having a secure job with a guaranteed income
- Their belief that they are the one taking all the risks
- Their sense that their staff don't work as hard as they do

Try to show them that you are both on the same page

The best way to defuse this potential mindset is to get in there first and acknowledge their position. Show them that you understand why you have to earn your keep. That you respect what they've achieved and how they've achieved it. That you want to help the company to earn more money so you can both benefit from it.

You can do this in your introduction to the meeting

As you explain why you asked for the meeting, tell your boss that you want to be sure that your contribution is translating into genuine business value.

That you know the time you spend on these things is coming from their pockets. You see it as their personal money and hence you never want to waste any of it.

Just before you introduce your research, tell them how much respect you have for them having built and run a business. You can only imagine how much time and effort they have had to put in over the years. You know you couldn't do it.

If your boss starts to open up about the effort they put in then let them. Enjoy the moment, park any preconceptions, and if you are genuinely impressed you should tell them.

Not all business owners will open up, but if yours does you should treat it as a privilege. A golden opportunity for you to build a stronger relationship with them.

I do realise not every business owner fits this description

Some business owners have little ego, others lack confidence. Many are incredibly generous to their staff. Just know that all of them will have put blood, sweat and tears into building their businesses.

Chapter 13

HOW CAN I GET MORE THAN THE NORMAL GOING RATE?

Feeling greedy? It is possible to negotiate for more, but this often involves a new role

===

Up until now, we have taken a wholly objective approach to judging how much you should ask for. At the same time, we have been managing your boss's emotions to lean more in your favour.

The main reason for choosing this particular approach is that almost anyone can make it work. You don't need any special negotiation or sales skills in order for it to be effective.

There is another reason for taking such a logical approach, though. It's because your freedom to negotiate creatively has been limited by how well your company already knows you:

- They know your ability and how it has changed over time
- They know your role and what it means to the company
- They understand what your contribution is worth
- They have seen your personal development in real-time

So your boss has an awful lot of information to enable them to make an objective and calculated decision. It means they can judge confidently whether the specific contribution you are making right now is worth the increased pay you are asking for.

These, then, are very clear waters. To gain more negotiating freedom you need to muddy them a bit.

What would give you more negotiating power?

To give yourself the most negotiating freedom you are going to need two things in your favour. You want your employer to be both:

Unsure about:

- ✔ How much bigger your impact could be than they were initially imagining before they spoke to you

- ✔ How much further your role could develop if things go as well as they are now dreaming is possible

Excited about:

- ✔ Just how good an asset you could turn out to be for the business in the long-term

- ✔ The opportunity for the company's profitability to be increased thanks to your unique contribution

Employers who are both **unsure** and **excited** have a tendency to risk taking a punt when they are pushed to make a decision on the spot. They are just like the rest of us in that they can get caught up in the moment and let their enthusiasm get the better of them.

That tendency will give you far more scope to push your luck when you come to discuss your salary.

When are these situations likely?

It can occasionally happen at the company you already work for. If you have been offered a newly created role which you are the only person doing then that can give you this opportunity.

The company still knows you of course, but they are *unsure* of your potential in your new role. They were *excited* enough about the role to have wanted to create it. So those boxes are both ticked.

But your biggest opportunities tend to appear when you move to a new company. Just at the point they have offered you the job.

A new employer is going to offer you the biggest scope

They don't really know you yet. But they do know they want you.

If the role itself is also newly created then even better. We are now talking Unsure with a capital *"U"* and Excited with a capital *"E"*. Just how good a hire could you turn out to be? Your unique contribution could be just the magic the company needs.

Provided you recognise when they are properly hooked, this situation gives you a golden opportunity to exploit their desire to get hold of you.

This is the time to be super-positive and confident in your negotiating position. Show them your genuine excitement for the opportunity you can see for you to make a real difference to their business. That you are already thinking ahead to all the things you can achieve in this role.

Most importantly, keep building their excitement about the thought of hiring you to bring this new role to life. Then, when you feel the time is right, ask them to confirm the package they are offering. And get negotiating for what you really want.

Negotiating with a new employer? This is my method

This was never going to be a book about interview techniques. But I will tell you how I go about the final negotiation stage once it's clear that they are interested in offering me the position.

If I am getting the vibes that both the uncertainty and excitement criteria are in play, I ask them to confirm again the salary they are looking to offer me.

When I hear the figure I will quietly think for a bit, looking thoughtful.

I then come back with my tried and tested pitch:

"I was thinking more around £XX,000. I think that number better reflects what I can offer and the work that this role is going to need.

"You're going to know in just a few months if I am a good fit and if I am worth it. It will only have cost you an extra £Y,000 in that time to find out, which isn't such a big risk for you. But it will make a big difference to me.

"After that, if you feel that I'm not worth the extra money, then we can just call it quits. I won't be happy unless I am adding at least that much value anyway.

"The thing is, I would much rather start by knowing I am being paid what I am worth. That way I know I am going to be focusing all my energy into showing you exactly what I am capable of.

"And I really am excited about the value I can add here."

I used exactly this pitch the last time I interviewed for a role. And secured myself a 25% higher starting salary than the number we had been discussing up to that point.

That higher starting point then carried through every subsequent pay rise I received at the company, multiplying the benefit of my initial negotiation.

And yes, after those 3 months they were in no doubt that I was well worth the salary they were paying me.

Chapter 14

POWER WORDS AND PHRASES THAT PACK A SURPRISING PUNCH

In the heat of the moment you don't want to be searching for the right words. These will help to get your meeting back on-track

===

Sometimes you need to choose your words carefully to nudge your boss in the right direction without being heavy-handed about it.

Here is a small selection that I have found to be particularly powerful and effective over the years. Don't be tempted to over-use them but do keep them in mind. They are handy things to have in your pocket, ready to pull out should you need to.

"My contribution"
(*Brings the focus back to the overall value you bring to the business*)

"Really pleased"
(*Shows just the right amount of positivity and confidence in your position without being gushing*)

"Disappointed"
(*A great word if needed - not attacking or angry, but pointed all the same*)

"Thank You"
(*Look them in the eyes and say "thank you" properly, so they know that you mean it*)

"I never want to be greedy, I just need to know I am being paid fairly. The going rate is all I'm ever going to ask for."

(*If your boss is looking dubious at your suggested figure*)

"I know that getting paid less than I am worth is going to eat away at me. And I really don't want that."

(*"Eat away at me" is really powerful. Don't demotivate a great employee*)

"I don't want to waste a load of energy stressing about or resenting my salary - I want to stay excited and positive. I need to be focusing all my energy on doing a great job."

(*This is useful if your boss generally agrees with your position but is hesitating on how high your salary request is*)

BECAUSE I'M WORTH IT

Chapter 15

WHATEVER YOU DO, DON'T DO THESE

Any one of these major gaffes could see your chances of a pay rise go up in smoke

===

✗ Don't come over as aggressive

No-one wants to feel bullied and especially not by someone they are supposed to be managing. Remember, you want your boss to be on your side. To genuinely want to give you a higher salary and not to resent the very idea of it.

For that to happen they need to feel relaxed and in control of the situation. Push them hard and they are going to push back.

✗ Don't brag about the great pay rise you just negotiated

Do you think the company wants everyone to know they can be talked into paying you more? What do you think would happen next? And then the next time you ask for a pay rise?

I can tell you from experience that when an employee does this you rapidly stop feeling warm and fuzzy about giving them their pay rise. You only let them burn you once.

✘ **Don't use someone else's pay rise as a lever**

See above. If someone at work has given you all the details about their pay rise then more fool them. Feel free to store it internally as useful intelligence, but nothing more.

Used as a lever it will just get your colleague in hot water. It won't gain you a raise. Both of you will have just gone downhill in your boss's estimation.

✘ **Don't be insincere**

When praising others or telling your boss how much they have helped you, you have to mean it. Find something you can say sincerely or don't say anything. Trust me, people can tell.

The funny thing about genuinely praising others is that it tends to reflect well on you as well as on them. Just the fact that you are recognising and sharing someone else's qualities somehow has a way of linking you to the value of that quality.

✘ **Don't fail to follow through**

If there are any conditions attached to your pay rise and you agreed to them then you need to keep your end of the bargain. Don't just relax and hope they will forget. Bosses and HR departments rarely do.

Companies are perfectly entitled to remove your pay rise in this situation and to demand any extra they have paid you back. I've seen it happen.

✘ **Don't make it all about you and your problems**

Bottom line, your needing more money is not adding value to the company. And loading your problems onto your boss is not making their life easier.

It may buy you some sympathy on a personal level but it isn't going to get you your pay rise. Keep your eyes on the prize.

✘ **Don't make figures and achievements up**

I cannot believe how often this happens. Like they won't check. Or don't know the numbers themselves. Or will somehow forget what you said when the truth eventually comes out.

All trust is out the window when you do this. No matter how good the rest of your work, there will always be the suspicion that it shouldn't be taken at face value.

✘ **Don't snatch defeat from the jaws of victory**

Sometimes things actually go way better than expected. The moment you open your mouth in your meeting, your boss beats you to the punchline and tells you they are raising your salary to almost exactly what you were looking for.

That's obviously fantastic news. But what about all your research, the pitch you've prepared, your contribution examples? **Forget about them!**

Don't plough on regardless. Just smile and say *"Thank you, I really appreciate that"* and say it like you mean it.

I know you've put a lot of effort into your preparation, but you've just won your big prize. So don't say or do anything now that could jeopardise it.

PLAN OF ACTION TEMPLATE

This is your planning list: all the key things you need to do, placed in the right order

===

1. Write down your "Why you're worth it" list

What's changed about your contribution that means you should now be getting paid more?

2. Get a feeling for the key players

Understand their likely drivers and identify any hurdles you are going to have to manage.

3. Make it easy for your boss

Give them the ammunition and the motivation to want to help you. Be the employee they'd love to clone.

4. Look at any hurdles you have identified and decide your strategy for how to tackle them

Issues with key players? Restrictive pay structure? Something else? Work out your plan to get around it.

5. Do your "going rate" research

Get online and gather your salary range evidence. Determine where your salary should sit within that range and why.

6. Check your timing

Is now a good time to ask for more money or would it be wiser to wait a little longer?

7. Set things up the week before your meeting

Get all your ducks in a row, complete your preparation and then book the meeting with your boss.

8. The big day - having the conversation with your boss

You're well prepared now, so summon your inner confidence, wear a smile and nail that pay rise!

9. Follow up

Keep any promises you have made and hold your boss to theirs.

BECAUSE I'M WORTH IT

Chapter 16

A PLAN IS NO USE WITHOUT THE ACTION BIT

Time to get started. Take the first step now and the rest should come easy to you

===

Remember the second statistic from the very start of this book?

Over two thirds of people who ask for a pay rise do successfully get one

Well, you can be sure that most of them won't have prepared anywhere near as well as you are going to. So take confidence and inspiration from knowing both their successes and all the effort you are going to put in.

Now it's time to stop putting off asking the big question. It's time instead for you to **start taking action**.

The best time for you to start is right now

Yes, literally right now. Before you put this book down and get distracted elsewhere. As with anything that's a little scary or involves a bit of effort, your biggest challenge is simply starting.

So I'm going to make that easy for you. Grab yourself a piece of paper and a pen, or your phone or tablet. And start writing down your reasons for "*Why you're worth it*".

Bingo. You've started. Now go back to the Plan of Action Template (page 137), and set yourself some deadlines to complete each task. Commit yourself to doing them and you're on a roll.

If you need a bit of additional motivation, write down the things you would do with the extra money a pay rise would bring. How good would it make you feel? What difference would it make to your quality of life?

Most of all, don't let yourself be intimidated by the very idea of asking for the pay rise you deserve.

Instead, be empowered by it.

You've got this

Because you're worth it

BECAUSE I'M WORTH IT

Chapter 17

TROUBLESHOOTING GUIDE

Life isn't always simple, but that shouldn't stop us from getting the things we deserve

===

Thankfully most salary conversations are straightforward. But just in case yours turns out not to be, these troubleshooting tips are here to help you to get things back on-track.

If someone higher up in the company doesn't like you

If you suspect this is the case and that person is influential to one of the key players (or worse, they *are* one of the key players themselves) then there are two things you can do about it:

First, you should build your reputation as widely as possible in the company (see '*Hurdle 1*' on the following page) so this person's negative view of you will stand out as being out of sync with the wider opinion.

Second, you can raise your concerns about that person when you have your pay rise conversation with your manager. Ask your boss if there is anything you can do to improve the situation and if there is any way they could help you to resolve it.

If your boss doesn't get on with their own boss

If you suspect this is the case then you have two extra hurdles to get over:

Hurdle 1 - It may not be enough for your boss to think that you are great, as their boss may not trust their opinion

This is the easier of the two to deal with, as long as you aren't totally isolated from the rest of the company. This is because you need to make yourself visible. The key is to make sure that other managers (and ideally your boss's boss) can see first-hand just how good you are.

If you get the opportunity, look to do some great work for managers other than your boss. Talk to them whenever you get the chance. Ask them intelligent questions about the business.

Believe me, managers talk to each other and share views on who they think the rising stars are.

Hurdle 2 - Your boss may be wary of rocking the boat

This is less likely to be a problem if your boss knows for sure that you are highly regarded by others (see above). If anything, they have more to lose if they don't keep you happy and then their boss finds out.

So concentrate on clearing Hurdle 1 first. Once you are confident that other managers see you in a positive light, then you can apply some gentle pressure to your boss. (see the "Power Words" section on page 129 for some useful phrases to help)

If you have a boss who takes all your credit

There are few things more annoying in life than watching your boss take all the credit for your hard work and expertise. To handle this situation, the first thing to do is to ensure that other managers know what work you do, how well you do it, and how to recognise it as being yours.

Try using "signature" turns of phrase and styling elements in your work that unmistakably come across as being from you. Seek out the people your boss has been sharing your work with. Not to complain about your boss's behaviour, though. The trick is to be subtle about it. Instead, ask them what they thought about *your* work and if they have any questions *for you*. People aren't stupid and they will normally work it out sooner or later.

What if doing this isn't enough?

The very worst bosses are the ones who believe that taking credit for your work is absolutely key to maintaining their own position. They fear what would happen to them if the truth came out.

Bosses like this desperately want to keep you but don't want to promote you in a way that would mean they lose personal access to the work that you are producing (and they are taking credit for).

If you find yourself in this situation, ask yourself if you really want to stay working for this person? If you don't (and personally I wouldn't) then there isn't so much risk in taking your own direct action. Go and see their manager, or the HR department if that feels more comfortable. Tell them it is a delicate matter and explain what's been happening. Be clear that you like the company but you need to be working for a different boss.

Or you could take the plunge and start looking for a job (and your pay rise) elsewhere in a less toxic environment.

If your boss would be earning less than you

This happens more often than you might think. In truth, this shouldn't really be an issue. Many managers (and even CEOs) have staff working for them who are paid more than they are.

This comes back to the logic of using the "going rate for your contribution" when considering salaries. Your specialism and your expertise may be rare, valuable and highly sought after. If your employer wants access to it then they have to pay accordingly.

Regardless of your salary, your manager would still be your manager. You are still going to respect them in just the same way and listen to what they ask you to do. It just happens that the going rate for your skills are currently higher than the going rate for theirs.

If your boss does bring this up then that is how I would recommend explaining your view to them. Remember, your boss needs to feel in control and, like anyone, they want to feel good about themselves. Help them to see that your pay rise isn't going to be a threat to either of these things.

What would complicate things is if your boss is also being underpaid right now

It takes a lot to openly admit this situation to one of your staff, as you can imagine. So if your boss is open about their salary situation with you then it's a good sign that you have a positive and trusting relationship with them.

This transparency now gives you an opportunity to work together to help each other. Just as your research has shown you your going rate, similar research would show your boss theirs.

You could offer to do this research for them and suggest that you work together to get both of you the salaries you deserve.

BECAUSE I'M WORTH IT

If your boss says "We only give pay rises once per year"

This is simply a brush-off so don't fall for it. Imagine your company had to replace you tomorrow at exactly your level of ability. What salary would they have to offer to attract and keep your replacement? Don't you think that's precisely what they would do?

The way to handle this:

Make the point that your development means you are no longer doing the same work at the same level that you were at the last annual pay rise date.

Remind your manager that waiting for the next annual increase would mean your putting up with being underpaid for X months. And you have no guarantee that your pay would be increased to a fair amount at that point.

In the meantime you know that the feeling of being undervalued would start to eat away at you. And you don't want to start resenting the company every time your payslip arrives. Because sooner or later you know you will get fed up enough to look elsewhere and you really don't want it to come to that.

If your boss says there's no money available for pay rises right now

This may actually be true, so the first thing to do is to look for clues as to how honest your boss's claim is:

- Is the company boasting about its successes or warning about low sales and downturns?

- Are they throwing lavish staff events or noticeably drawing their horns in?

- Is the senior management team all smiles or either absent or looking increasingly stressed?

If you have hard evidence that actually there is plenty of money around then you should mention it. But do tread carefully. Your boss is not going to enjoy being called out as a liar if they told you this straight to your face.

One approach to try is this: "*I understand, but I think mine is an exceptional case. And I heard recently that...*" Then explain what is giving you the impression that money isn't so tight that they couldn't afford to pay you fairly for your work.

What if you think there probably *is* no money right now?

Well, if that is the case it's either going to be a temporary cashflow situation or a longer-term issue. The latter isn't good. Because let's face it, failing companies aren't great for your career progression.

So I would ask your boss straight up which of the two it is. Then if you think there is still a future for the business, try this approach: "*That's obviously disappointing to hear but thank you for being honest with me.*" Then negotiate forwards.

To do this, see if you can get your boss to agree that you are worth the money you are asking for. And that as soon as the company is back on its feet they will revisit your salary. Then put a date in the diary to follow it up.

If you are feeling a bit cheeky, you could try to negotiate something that won't affect their cashflow in the meantime. For example you could ask for some extra days off in lieu until the company is in a position to increase your pay.

If you got into an argument

Hopefully you have already read the "Whatever you do, don't do these" chapter (page 133) so you will be trying very hard to avoid this. But if an argument does happen don't beat yourself up too much. We've all been there. Myself included, despite my best efforts. The good news being that I also knew how to apologise.

Which is exactly what you should do now and quickly. As soon as you have both calmed down, go back and say sorry. Even if you think it was all your boss's fault, you should apologise for reacting so strongly. Trust me, your boss won't be feeling particularly proud of themselves at this moment either. So if you can get to the point where you both smile at each other, then well-recovered.

Ask to re-book your meeting and tell your boss you would like to hear their side again. That you know there is a reason they reacted the way they did and you would like to learn from it.

Take your research back in with you at that meeting and calmly try again.

What if your boss is just a total a**e?

Sadly, they do exist. In fact we've probably all met at least one of them in our lives. But ask yourself, do you really want to be working for one? It may be tempting to just put up with the situation and keep taking the money. But a toxic environment is more than just a bit draining. It can actually lead to severe health implications.

So think hard. Is the money they pay you really worth it? Especially if you believe that you are getting less than the going rate for the work that you do. If you have completed your salary research then you will doubtless have seen other comparable roles to your current one. Roles that might suit you. Where your toxic boss won't be a part of your life.

Tell me, is this really the only company you could work for? Personally, I'd be voting with my feet.

BECAUSE I'M WORTH IT

Reality check - just how well did these techniques work for me?

It's one thing for me to talk about these as principles but what about the numbers themselves? What was my strike rate like? How much more did I earn by finding the courage to ask for a pay rise whenever I felt I deserved one?

The difference that asking made to my income

Being a Brit, I still find it hard to talk openly about money. It just isn't the done thing, even now. I also have to consider the impact of my career path on the numbers as many of my pay rises were the consequence of moving up the corporate ladder. For these reasons I don't think it would be helpful to show you all my salaries. In fact, it could be misleading.

Instead I am going to estimate the difference that asking for a pay rise (or a higher salary when changing jobs) has made to my take-home earnings over the years. Compared to following the same career path but simply accepting whatever salary was offered.

Having looked back at 27 years of my working life, I can identify at least twelve times that I asked for more than was on the table. I was successful eleven of those times. The twelfth? That was after the 2008 financial crisis had hit the business harder than I realised and I was told bluntly "there is no money". I believed my boss when he said that and took it on the chin. Then I tried again later that year when business looked up and I got what I asked for.

I have calculated that, by asking for more whenever I felt it was the right thing to do, I increased my total take-home earnings by over 70%. I also negotiated extra paid time off, a better pension, flexible working hours and, back when they were a perk, a decent company car. All by asking at the right time in the right way.

BECAUSE I'M WORTH IT

ABOUT THE AUTHOR

I've got a confession to make. I hate writing about myself. Most "about the author" sections may be written in the 3rd person but don't be fooled. Nine times out of ten it is still the author doing the writing. I tried that approach initially and I found it horrible. So I am going to drop any pretence here and just write it as me. It's my book, after all.

Where to start? I'm what is becoming increasingly known as a generalist. Go back a few years and you might have called me a jack of all trades. Which can be a bit of a pain when someone asks me exactly what it is that I do. Solve problems, mainly, I guess. Whenever I see an issue I just want to sort it. I can't help myself.

When I first started out, most of these problems were technical in nature. Then over time they became more strategic, communication-related and cultural. It turns out I have a knack for analysing systems and developing people. As well as managing the complex web of relationships that forms between them.

Short version? Started in the construction industry as a CAD Operator and finished as Marketing Manager, having won multiple awards in areas I had no background in. Then swapped a career in plasterboard for a career in pensions (yep, I know an exciting industry when I see one), leaving when I was the Commercial Director of one of the businesses I helped to grow.

I have battled against social anxiety, raced a Caterham, travelled, cooked and almost certainly taken the record for the slowest progression from beginner to intermediate guitar player. And now I have finally written a book.

BECAUSE I'M WORTH IT

INDEX

accounts, 23, 30
ad-hoc rises, 44, 52, 61
adjusting, 73, 76
agent (recruitment), 37, 38
aggressiveness, 134
agreements, 93, 106
ambitions, 34
anchoring, 67–72, 76
apologising, 152
arguments, 100, 152
Ariely (Dan), 69
attendance, 22, 23
attitude, 18, 89, 112

bands (salary), 44
bargain, 69, 71–73, 92, 107, 135
barriers, 4, 10, 73
basic pay, 51
behaviour, 84, 85, 148
believing, 10
bidding, 69, 70
blaming, 58
blockers, 45
bonuses, 48, 49
booking, 38, 78, 84, 85, 107

bragging, 134
brush-off, 107, 150
budget, 24, 46, 47, 65, 66, 110
bullied, 134
business-critical, 39
business owner, 120, 121

candidates, 37, 40
capability, 91
career, 6, 7, 34, 52, 61, 63, 112, 114, 116, 151, 155, 157
carrot and stick, 48
cashflow, 151, 152
checklist, 56
Chris (Voss), 93
clients, 31, 57
colleagues, 5, 6, 31, 39, 46, 47, 63, 83, 106
commission-only, 50, 51
competence, 4, 37, 44, 101
complaining, 148
conditions, 78, 79, 135
confidence, 10, 130
confrontational, 101
consistency, 22, 42

INDEX

costs, 23, 24, 32, 36–38, 78
courage, 3, 114, 155
courses, 33, 65
credibility, 99

deadlines, 107, 142
decision-maker, 21, 84
defensive, 73, 110
delicate matter, 148
director, 24, 103, 157
disappointed, 107, 130
disputes, 31
disruptive, 3, 7, 36, 40
drivers, 18, 19, 21, 28, 107, 113, 138

earn, 7, 14, 48, 55, 63, 122, 155
economists, 69
emotional, 5, 29, 30, 86, 120
emotions, 5, 110, 112, 114, 124
energy, 34, 58, 84, 128, 131
evidence, 5, 24, 55, 57, 60, 73, 85, 91, 139, 151

face-to-face, 99
fairness, 42
family, 90, 121
fatigue, 84
fear, 23, 148
feedback, 6, 33, 113, 114

feelings, 33
finance director, 24
focus, 50, 72, 73, 128, 131
following-up, 111
freedom, 2, 7, 45, 62, 124, 125

gaffes, 134
goals, 3, 5, 52
greed, 58, 124, 131
gross misconduct, 36
growth, 13, 34

habits, 39, 84
headhunters, 37
health impact, 153
healthcare, 65
hiring, 13, 37–40, 52, 126
honesty, 56, 76, 102, 151
hostage negotiator, 93
HR department, 22, 23
hurdles, 20, 22, 52, 73, 108, 138, 146, 147

impact, 30, 54, 57, 91, 93, 95, 97, 117, 125
income, 48, 51, 121, 155
inductions, 36, 38
inflation, 116
insecurities, 3
insincerity, 135

INDEX

interviews, 36, 38
introvert, 84
irreplaceable, 37

language, 8, 20, 30
laws (employment), 36
learning, 102, 106
leverage, 50
listening, 102, 110
location, 4, 101
Loewenstein (George), 69
logic, 4, 5, 70, 120, 149
loophole, 42, 44

magic, 68, 126
management, 23, 151
margins, 13
Massachusetts IoT, 69
metrics, 23
mindset, 18, 50, 89, 120–22
misconduct, 36
motivation, 19, 26, 33, 34, 55, 63, 138, 143

negative, 23, 54, 113, 146
negotiation, 67, 68, 111, 124, 127, 128
nervousness, 114
numbers, 29, 30, 50, 72, 136, 155

objections, 18
onboarding, 40
opportunity, 14, 47, 52, 80, 107, 112, 113, 122, 126, 149
options, 24, 49, 51, 66, 82, 111, 114

package, 49, 65, 126
pain, 26, 36, 37, 40, 63, 157
paperwork, 36, 38
part-time, 61
payroll, 24, 45, 65
payslip, 106, 108, 150
pay structures, 41-52
pension, 65, 155
performance, 19, 23, 26, 27, 33, 39, 49, 54, 112
pitch, 18, 47, 85, 89, 99, 101, 127, 128, 136
plan, 29, 69, 94, 108, 138, 142
plan of action template, 137
power, 2, 3, 58, 69, 72, 125
power words and phrases, 129
praising, 78, 135
preparation, 12, 20, 21, 82, 83, 111, 136, 139
professionality, 102, 114
projects, 30, 40, 78
promises, 106, 139
punishment scheme, 49

161

INDEX

ranges (salary), 71, 72
rates (going), 38, 56
reactions, 36, 114, 120
recruitment, 23, 37, 38
relaxed, 79, 85, 90, 97, 99–101, 134
remote, 65, 99
reputation, 40, 64, 146
risk, 21, 37, 39, 51, 114, 121, 125, 127, 148
rules, 7, 22, 23, 42, 43, 45, 52, 62, 69

sales, 18, 32, 48, 50, 78, 79, 92, 124, 151
script, 83, 88
self-assessment, 91
self-belief, 10
self-interest, 28
self-worth, 2, 114
shareholders, 13
silence, 102
skills, 4, 7, 50, 52, 56, 58, 113, 116, 124, 149
sleep, 86
specialism, 149
specialist, 6, 32, 37, 43, 52, 60, 76
special sauce, 54, 57
stalling, 107
star (employee), 31, 63
students, 69, 70

targets, 13, 19, 20, 60, 61, 63, 64
technology, 13, 69
template, 137
timescales, 104, 107
timing, 45, 46, 52, 78, 82, 84, 110, 139
tone, 90, 97
training, 31, 36, 38, 65
transparency, 149
troubleshooting, 146
trust, 86, 100, 136, 147

underpaid (being), 149, 150
undervalued (feeling), 150
unionised industry, 7
unsure, 125, 126

valuable, 3, 43, 52, 57, 116, 149
visuals, 99
Voss (Chris), 93

wages, 2, 6, 48, 61, 71
waiting, 24, 79, 150
wastage, 32
wellbeing, 66
what salary to ask for, 59

Yougov, 2

Printed in Great Britain
by Amazon